# YOU ACTUALLY CAN H

and you can start any time. Chara Davis learned that the hard way after years of feeling victimized. But learn it she did and she shares her story, her revelations, and her truth in hopes of inspiring others going through their own toughest of times.

What Chara tells—holding nothing back—is the story of her life. For a number of reasons it was not an easy one. It went from happy and content to being dark and dismal literally overnight.

It started when Chara was just four and her mom became very ill. It went downhill from there. She was shuffled off to relatives and family friends, one of whom was a child abuser. But who would believe a little kid?

As things became more difficult and dysfunctional, Chara became increasingly troubled and overweight. Disrupted dreams were her lot. In her late thirties a recovery center located in Malibu California would save her life.

While neither an alcoholic nor an addict, Chara was able to gain admittance to a program that addressed her childhood trauma and put her on a path that not only changed her future, it changed the way she saw—and related to—her past.

How Chara approached her recovery will open your eyes to new possibilities for yourself. Even better, who she has become will inspire you to reach for them.

There are many things to be gained from this book. If you approach what Chara says with neutrality and an open mind, you can free yourself from viewing your past as a forever imprint of heartache, darkness and failure. Let go of what drags you down and start to recognize your own disguised blessings so you can propel yourself into a bright and happy future.

# ABOUT THE AUTHOR

**Chara Davis** has had more than her share of
trials in this life. But you'd never know it today.
She struggled through family dysfunction and
being abused starting around the age of nine,
and endured an overweight and self-destructive
adolescence. Then, in her late thirties she found
a way to turn her life around, literally recreating her view of her past
and creating a new and highly promising future.

Chara is now happily married, the mother of three spectacular
children, and prospering in a career that assists people in becoming
fit and healthy. Chara lives with her husband and three children in
Bloomsburg, Pennsylvania.

# DISGUISED BLESSINGS

# DISGUISED BLESSINGS

One woman's inspiring
story of transformation
and a model for reclaiming
**YOUR** life

# CHARA DAVIS

OUR LEGACY
PUBLISHING

BLOOMSBURG, PA

Our Legacy Publishing
88 Hidlay Church Road
Bloomsburg, PA 17815

Printed in the United States of America

*Publisher's Cataloging-In-Publication*

Names: Davis, Chara, author.
Title: Disguised blessings : one woman's inspiring story of transformation and
a model for reclaiming your life / Chara Davis.
Description: Bloomsburg, PA : Our Legacy Publishing, [2016] | Includes index.
Identifiers: ISBN: 978-0-9982171-0-9 (pbk.) | 978-0-9982171-1-6 (eBook)
| LCCN: 2016917101
Subjects: LCSH: Davis, Chara. | Self-help techniques. | Adult children of
dysfunctional families--Personal narratives. | Adult child sexual
abuse victims--Personal narratives. | Psychic trauma in adolescence
--Treatment--Personal narratives. | Recovery movement--Personal
narratives. | Self-actualization (Psychology) | Self-acceptance. | Self-
realization. | Self-esteem. | Attitude (Psychology) | Quality of life.
| LCGFT: Autobiographies.
Classification: LCC: BF637.S4 D38 2016 | DDC: 158.1--dc23

Book Shepherd: Ellen Reid
Cover Design: Lewis Agrell
Interior Design: Ghislain Viau
Author Photo Page 109: Studio D photography, Eddie Donlin
Other Author Photos: Michelle Fitz Photography

# CONTENTS

# INTRODUCTION

I have felt a very strong push to tell my story to others, because it shows we have the power to realize that change is possible. It graphically demonstrates that what we tell ourselves today is what really matters—NOT where we were yesterday!

My story is real, honest, and true. I no longer have hate, resentment, or anger toward anyone from past events. My heart has forgiven, and I am at peace. My anger is understood and controlled. I am, for the first time, happy and content with the person I fought so hard to become. I am thankful for all the good, bad, and in-between events because they have made me who I am today: strong, capable of anything, and thankful that I am blessed.

In my late thirties, a few life-changing events forced me to open the door to my past and unlock all of the horrible incidents that had taken place in my younger years. I was determined to find the answers and make the change. So I did.

My addictions would surface into my life, one way or another. When I say "addiction," I am not speaking of hard street drugs and/or alcohol. My addictions included food, sugar, diet pills, laxatives, exercise, nicotine, and toxic relationships. I eventually got so sick and tired of my own bullshit that I took all necessary steps required to change.

I had longed for a better life; I simply didn't understand at the time that the determining factor was inside of me. I finally discovered that no one could do it for me. I would need to save myself. I had to start making better choices, because my life and future depended on what I chose to do from here on out.

It was time for me to stop making excuses and take action. I had been taking the easy way out every day, but I was suffering because of my daily choices.

In my early twenties, I had begun intensively researching health and fitness. I studied hard and tried, time after time, to find a program that worked. Finally, in my late thirties, I came up with a formula that would not only change my life, my physical appearance, and my mental health—but it also began changing the lives of others who implemented my programs. It was transformational! I no longer needed anti-anxiety or anti-depressant drugs.

I began making better lifestyle choices (sometimes slowly, but continuously) that felt right and good to me. My life completely opened up and became a lot more FUN, happy, and meaningful. Those right choices—which we CAN make each day—will set us free.

None of this means that I'm "perfect" when it comes to diet or exercise, but my life changed drastically once I was able to control my food and exercise. I am healthier and happier than I have ever been. Now that I have control over my addictions, I understand that everything I put into my body will affect my mood, energy, health, and ultimately my quality of life. I began to heal my entire being from the inside out. I knew the exterior appearance would fall into place once I was able to manage my emotions and figure out why my life had been so unmanageable.

We all make choices, and we are capable of turning our lives around and making changes in order to be genuinely happy. It does not matter where we come from, what we have done in our past, or how far "gone" we think we are. None of that will ever matter. What matters most are the choices we make today.

It's never too late. The truth within can set us free, and it can even help us inspire others. And that's why I am writing this book.

I have come to the realization that nothing anyone does is really about *us*. If we can allow the actions of others to slip by—and if we can manage to not take them personally—our lives can become our own. In understanding this, I have also discovered what *I* do is never about *anyone else*. What I do is all about finding satisfaction for myself.

Accomplishment and discovery come from the choices we make. It's about seeking and expressing yourself and the resulting emotions that are evoked. If you give kindness and positivity, you will be consumed with happiness and a genuine sense of self-worth. If you display unkind and hurtful behaviors to another, you will become consumed with hate and disappointment.

Others are just mirrors showing us what our actions really look like. We are what we are surrounded by; we become the reflection that is displayed. For example, when you lend a helping hand to someone, the expression from the person you are helping is displayed as a grateful smile. That smile fills your heart with meaning and purpose, which is a direct reflection of that specific action. Conversely, if you cause harm to another in the physical form or attempt to alter their emotional well-being, you will see an expression of rejection, judgment, and ridicule that makes your heart sad.

Life is about seeking to express yourself with an understanding that emotions are evoked. We can see reflected in others the emotions we feel within ourselves. "We reap what we sow."

The reality is, we all have the power to choose how to express ourselves. Once the expression is transformed into action, we watch it reflected back to us. This means our own actions have a positive or negative impact on our lives.

I dedicate my story to those who have lost all hope for a better life. If you feel stuck in a world that moves on without you, it is time to get up and get moving! I spent years being misunderstood and rejected, only to find out it was me who had the power to change the outcome of my life all along. The same is true for you.

I wish all of you the best of luck on your journey!

# CHAPTER ONE

# REJECTED AND ABANDONED

"As I look back on my life, every time I thought I was being REJECTED from something good, I was actually being REDIRECTED to something better."

The older I get, the more I find myself reflecting on days, weeks, and years that have passed by. I think, "Why did I?" or even "How could I?" Many years ago, someone told me, "Bad choices make for great stories, right?" I never found comfort in this statement, but it has proven to be the truth.

Along with all the amazing things that have happened in my life, I can't help but reflect on the mistakes I made along the way: the things that went really wrong, the things I wish I could have done better, and the things I wish I would never have done. Regret used to determine how each day would begin and how each day would end.

I understand now that, if it were not for the errors and poor judgment, I would not have learned how to "reframe" my thoughts and control my actions. But I used to hold onto those painful experiences and tell myself what an idiot I was. As someone who used to be the biggest self-doubter around, I know how easy it can be to inadvertently slip into that kind of "down on yourself" thought process. It was something I had to unlearn.

How we talk about ourselves and see ourselves is a practice, just like our weekly workout schedule is a practice. Repeating any practice over time forms a habit … and habits lead to outcomes and results, good or bad.

No one wants to wake up and say, "I think I'll screw up today." But even our subconscious negative thoughts produce negative behaviors. Instead of viewing yourself as the victim, it's important to "reframe" your thoughts so you can see yourself as a good person who was involved in some pretty shitty events.

Be your own hero. Rise from the darkness and overcome all the past hurt and pain. Don't blame others. Stop playing the victim. Own your mistakes and believe you are worthy and capable of having a good life with good people in it, no matter what you've done. You must practice self-love and forgiveness in order to prevail.

Recognize, love, and honor yourself as a gift from God. We are not our mistakes. Why do we fall? So we can learn to pick ourselves up again.

It's easier said than done, but one thing I've learned for sure is that it NEVER gets easier. WE just get better! The irony of life is that the more we make mistakes, the more we can learn. Don't waste another minute wallowing in darkness. Own your failures, find the lessons, and keep moving so you can make the most of your life.

REMEMBER that the REASON YOU ARE HERE living your life is because you are one of God's greatest gifts. When you're ready, you will eventually get sick and tired of your own BS. Then you can open to the awareness that everything that's come before was an important part of your journey, and that TODAY, you are EXACTLY WHERE YOU ARE SUPPOSED TO BE.

That's what finally happened to me—and I needed help to get there. I'm offering that kind of help to you with this book.

In my early childhood years I never really understood what contentment meant. I was unsure of many people, places, and things. I had no clue what it felt like to wake up and not have an overwhelming feeling of anger, fear, and sadness. Everything was so dark and miserable all the time, and it all began at the very young age of four years old.

Looking back on my previous life, I am grateful for everything I endured and all of the challenges I faced.

Looking forward, I'm filled with vision. Looking upwards, I am filled with strength. Looking within, I am now filled with peace.

But at the age of four, I was not any of those things.

Over thirty-five years later, I can still remember the events that took place that would alter my entire being and lead me down a path of constant self-sabotaging, destructive behavior. I don't really remember much before that time, but for some reason, I can remember *everything* from then on out.

I remember waking up on a normal Saturday morning. My father was in the service and was stationed overseas, so Saturdays were special times for my mother and some of our other relatives to go on fun outings. But instead of my mother bustling around the house getting things ready, it was strangely quiet. Family members had been arriving, one by one, and things became stranger with each new body that entered my home. My mother's bedroom was quickly filled with fifteen or more relatives and friends, but no one would let me in.

I sat on the doorstep waiting to hear my mom yell that we were leaving, but she never did. The minutes turned into hours, and I still had no idea what was going on in my mother's bedroom. Every time I would ask someone, I would be shushed and shuffled off to the side. So I stayed busy trying to keep my two-year-old sister comforted and quiet. She was crying for my mother, and I felt like crying, too. But I was the big sister and had to put on a brave front for her. Thankfully, she was easy to distract. Over the years, comforting and reassuring her became my main role with her. I made myself the buffer, protecting her from all of the frightening events and abuse that I would endure in the years to come.

Eventually, I was able to sneak to my mother's bedroom and sneak a peek at what was going on. I will never forget the scene I witnessed.

My mother lay still, unable to move. Drool was sliding out of both corners of her mouth. The hands that used to comb my hair were crippling before my eyes, curled up like little balls and tucked under her armpits. The legs she used to dance around with in our living room, singing with a comb she used for her microphone, were shaking uncontrollably. Everyone in her bedroom kept repeating her name as they shook her, trying to get her limp body to stand. They were begging for her to say anything that would give them hope that there was still life within her still body.

I heard our neighbor calling for an ambulance, but it made no sense as she began to explain my mother's condition. Many times throughout my childhood, I would remember this day. I would wake up with tears running down my cheeks after I dreamed of searching for my mother during the night. These nightmares would continue throughout my adult life.

As soon as my grandmother spotted me, she guided me out of the doorway and into my uncle's car, and I was immediately taken away—away from my mother.

My sister and I sat in the back of my uncle's car, sobbing. We were so scared about what was happening to our mother. I could not find the strength to comfort my sister at that moment, because I felt like I was falling apart. I was shaken by what I had just witnessed. Those visions from her bedroom will never leave my memory.

This would be the last time I would see my mother for many days. I had so many questions, but no one was talking about my mother's condition. My pleas were quickly dismissed. My sister and I were treated like a problem rather than a priority during this crisis.

As the hours grew into days and the days turned into weeks, I grew angrier and more frustrated. I started throwing tantrums and doing anything I could to get someone to pay attention to me. But nobody would explain where my mother was. The only thing we were told was that she was not feeling well and we would see her soon. This was unacceptable. I wanted answers!

The anger grew strong very quickly. I felt rage in the form of physical pain for the first time in my young life. The silence, the secrets, the uncertainty of what the night would bring—not knowing was making me physically sick! I started throwing up, pulling my hair, and making tiny little scratches on my cheeks and arms. Creating this physical pain helped me get through the emotional pain of not seeing my mother for days. She left us without warning and I still had absolutely no explanation of why.

My sister and I were shuffled from relative to relative. We had no structure as we transitioned from house to house. Everyone had a new list of rules and activities. No matter who I asked, we would always hear the same explanation: my mother was unwell and we would see her soon. I really started to believe that she was gone and living in heaven. Nothing that was happening made sense to me. Why wouldn't they just let me see her?

My father was in the United States Army stationed in Germany during this time. Anyone who has been enlisted in the military understands it is not easy to be discharged. It can take days, weeks, and even months to be released. Thankfully, my father only had to wait a few weeks. My sister and I counted the days until his arrival home, hoping that our anxiety, anger, and feelings of abandonment would subside.

My father was only twenty years old when my mother became ill. They had both become parents at the very young age of sixteen. They were "babies" raising two babies of their own. One can imagine how overwhelming this would be for my father, at twenty, to have the responsibility of raising two small girls. Now he was hit with having to care for my mother and her debilitating disease as well.

My sister and I had been dealing with so many emotions while my father was gone. His being away was traumatic, creating extra stress for my mother, my sister, and me. When he left for Germany, my mother began to struggle with depression. She cried often. I remember feeling abandoned and confused.

Now I had mixed emotions about his returning home. I was angry, happy, sad, and hopeful all at the same time. When he walked through the door carrying his military bags, my sister and I bombarded him with hugs, tears, and kisses. Our dad was home! My father had always been my hero. My sister and I adored him so much. The circumstances at the time of his arrival were certainly not ideal, but at least now he was home. We were content with his presence.

As our father drove my sister and me to Winter Haven hospital, where my mother had been living for the past few weeks, I remember thinking everything would be better soon. We would all be a family and living back in our own home. I'd be sleeping in my very own bed again. But that dream was shattered the minute I saw my mother.

I was not prepared for what this young, vibrant woman had become. As a nurse wheeled my mother to the patio where we waited, I discovered just how fragile the human body could be.

What had the nurses and doctors done to my mom? This woman did not look, talk, or sound like the person I remembered. She had been full of life, energy, spunk, and personality. Now her eyes were covered with white patches and white tape. Her hands were still curled up in little balls and tucked under her armpits.

When she spoke, it sounded like a two-year-old was talking. Nothing she said made sense. We could not make out what she was trying to say. The voice that used to sing so beautifully and without effort was now mouthing scrambled words. She drooled as she tried to talk to us, and her sentences were not even words! What was this? What happened to my mother? I screamed so loudly, the nurses ran over to see what had happened and to make sure my mom was alright.

I looked up to see my father's eyes leaking tears. He was shaking so hard, he was not able to speak as he held me back. He was trying to conceal my loud yells as I screamed for my mother. My little mind and body were helpless, angry and scared to death about what was happening.

Many of us—possibly all of us—have experienced heartbreak, grief, or personal defeat that has stopped us dead in our tracks. During our darkest days, we begin to wonder how we will ever manage to move on past our current situation. If you have been there, you understand and have learned a thing or two about loss and loneliness. You will understand how all hope of "going back to normal" fled from me in that instant.

Hopelessness overwhelmed me to the point that, as the days passed, I would cry all the time, yet my tears just didn't flow. I began to sink into a very dark, depressed place. This would be a place that I would revisit many times during my life. Unfortunately, the sadness I felt as a child would always exist within me. I will never forget that day and how our family and our lives changed forever. The trauma from this experience would land me in therapy for many years.

As children, we look up to our parents—especially our mothers— for nourishment, protection, comfort, and emotional support. Mothers are the ones who make all the bad things go away and replace them with love and contentment. The good news is, I survived. My tenacious and hopeful spirit prevailed—despite the pain I had endured, beginning at the young age of four.

My mother's diagnosis ended up being Multiple Sclerosis. She had showed no signs of being ill up until the day she became paralyzed and unable to move. There had been no warning and no pain prior to the day she was removed from our home and taken away by ambulance. This disease destroyed my mother's brain, body, and speech within a few hours.

The cause of MS is unknown. It's a disease in which the body will attack itself, specifically the nerves in the brain, causing scars to form. The scars prevent the nerves from communicating as well as they should. Everyone who has been diagnosed with this disease progresses differently. The disease can affect the speech, brain, body mobility, and pain tolerance. My mother was twenty years old when MS descended upon her—and on all of us.

MS was not only my mom's disease; it became our family's disease. Later in my life, I would discover that my mother had experienced childhood trauma as well. She had unresolved issues that, on top of her disease, made it hard for her to care for us. She had known nothing but emotional pain from her childhood trauma, and now her disease was wearing down her body as well.

She spent months in the hospital undergoing therapy to relearn how to eat, talk, see, walk, and feed herself. Although my father was home now, my sister and I were passed along from relative to relative, never knowing who could take care of us next. When my father was not working, he spent all of his free time at the hospital with my mother. Our family decided the hospital was not the best place for children to be for that many hours every day.

When I was allowed to see my mom, I was unable to control my emotions. When it was time to leave, I screamed and cried, unwilling to let go of her. Everyone thought it was best for my mother's recovery if I visited as little as possible. My outbursts only upset her and could potentially slow down her remission.

Over the next few years, my mother continued to slip in and out of remission and in and out of the hospital. She was sick more than she was healthy. We were away from her more than we were with her.

My brother was born during one of her more serious relapses. His life was a true and honest miracle. We had moved from house to house and town to town, but eventually had moved in with my grandmother. My parents always had a volatile relationship. They fought day and night, mostly because my mother was unable to control her outbursts. She was a fighter and raged at my father. Mom and dad had been on the verge of divorce when my mother found out she was pregnant again.

The older I got, the angrier I became. All I wanted were parents who actually wanted to be a part of my life and who would spend time getting to know me. I desperately craved attention and a connection to my parents. I wanted to be validated for my existence on this earth. I would have loved to have my parents show up to a track meet, football game, dance recital, or anything that I was involved in, but they never came. I longed for the parent-child relationships I saw on my favorite television shows or witnessed in my friends' homes.

The sad truth is, my wish never came true during my childhood or teenage years. I went through life fending for myself, doing pretty much whatever I wanted to do. All three of us children were lost and alone. We spent many nights afraid of what each new day would bring. My mother's childhood trauma profoundly affected her parenting. Her explosive behavior eventually caused a physical sickness within me and molded the person I was going to become.

My sister, brother, and I searched for love and happiness outside of our home, because it certainly did not exist inside. All of our home lives revolved around my mother's depression and her illness.

The American novelist Ray Bradbury wrote: "You've got to jump off cliffs and build your own wings on the way down." This was what we had to do. This is how children survive growing up in an unstable environment.

Our lives felt crazy, scary, sad, chaotic, and meaningless. We woke up many nights with the noise of screaming, fighting, or partying with loud and obnoxious strangers in our home. Mom and Dad continued to fight all day and night. I would hear glass breaking and doors slamming. Sometimes, I would see my mother hitting my father. I would go into my sister's room at night and hug her so she would feel comfort and never be afraid.

As I lay next to her, crying without tears streaming from my eyes, I would also find comfort. We formed a bond that could never be broken. I found a sense of power, strength, and purpose while taking care of my siblings. At the same time, I also developed resentment toward them. Because I did not know how to express my emotions, they often came out in a physical form: screaming, yelling, throwing things, and raging until I no longer had the energy to move.

Even though I did everything and anything to keep my siblings from experiencing some of what I witnessed, they took the brunt of my emotional outbursts. They became frightened of my rage, even though it made me feel better to get the anger out.

Think about a pot of boiling water; that is how I would describe my temper at the time. My emotions would spill over into a fit of rage without any warning. Anything could trigger an outburst. A smell, a memory, a television show, a song on the radio—my anger always erupted without warning.

Throughout our childhood, our mother was in and out of the hospital more times than I can remember. We were shuffled around so many times, I lost count. But even when she was home in the physical sense, she was mentally checked out. Most of the time, she was unaware of anyone or anything around her. Her children were invisible.

When we were sent out of our home, I was always split up from my brother and sister because I was such a handful. To be honest, I had become bold, argumentative, and defiant. I fought with everyone and had little remorse for my bad behavior, so few people would take on the responsibility of caring for me while my mother was sick or in the hospital. My grandparents on both sides alternated often, but they were also trying to manage their own lives, my mother and father's lives, and the lives of their other children.

So I will admit, I was out of control and argumentative. I was mouthy, rude, and aggressive when I did not get my way. I felt a sense of entitlement, and being a badass was justification for the life I'd been handed.

At some point, my parents began sending me to stay with a certain individual. He became my caregiver on and off, whenever my mother was ill. Over the years, this man would have a huge impact on my life. He was a wealthy and respectable man in our community. Everyone but me looked up to him. This man was a relative who was married, with children of his own and prospering as a successful business owner.

Let's call him "Frank." Because of his success, he was well liked by doctors, lawyers, teachers, and even our town priest. He walked into a room and everyone wanted to talk to him. The sad thing is no amount of money will make you a good person. Frank had a way of making people like him. Luckily he was not around children on a daily basis. His children were grown and had families of their own at the time. When my parents placed me under his supervision, they were also placing me with his wife who had no idea what he was doing or what this man was capable of. *How can you not know?* I asked myself so many times throughout my life.

He was evil, sadistic, and liked to intimidate young girls. He made me do inappropriate things to him and forced me to watch him do disgusting sexual things to himself. This "respectable" man was arrogant enough to believe he was invincible and above all those who interacted with him. I was an innocent child.

He forced me to dress a certain way, eat what he made, and participate in anything he wanted me to do. He spoke to me as if I were worthless and treated me with no respect at all. He made me believe that no one cared about me but him.

His drunken outbursts and verbal abuse affected how I began to view myself. I can remember running out of his house and into the woods one night after he passed out from a long day of drinking. I was determined to escape and find my way home. I could not take one more derogatory remark, slap, or inappropriate gesture from this man. I can remember every sound and smell of the woods that night.

Once he discovered I was gone, he immediately came after me. I heard his dog barking as they searched. The closer they got to me, the more I regretted leaving the house. What had I been thinking? I prayed to God: if I couldn't go home, please just let me die.

He spanked me so hard, I could not sit down for days. The physical pain left an imprint not only on my body, but on my heart as well. I was deeply hurt. It had taken all the courage I had to set off into the woods. The fear of this experience will always exist within me.

He verbally threatened me, saying he would never let me go home. That scared me enough that I never tried to leave again. He made it very clear that, if I ever told anyone about what he was doing to me, I would never see my family again. I believed him.

Looking back on this, I know if I'd just had the courage to tell my parents, they would have never sent me there again. But I didn't trust them at the time.

The situation would play an enormous role in my life. I would struggle for years to set myself free from all the bad memories and abuse that I endured during my stays with that man.

The first time I was placed in the car with this person, who I barely knew at the time, I begged and pleaded with everyone not to send me. How could they send me away to stay with a stranger? I was so frightened, but nobody would listen. I was forced to go. My cries went unheard and my needs were quickly dismissed.

Sometimes, before they sent me back to him, I would pretend to be sick so I could stay home with my mother. No one would listen. I'd throw tantrums, scream, kick, and yell, but to no avail. I felt invisible because I was always forced to go, no matter how loud I could scream.

If I'd had the courage to tell my parents and my family what he did to me, my life would have been so different. But all I felt was fear and shame. I understood his threats. I was certain my family would blame me for the physical abuse I endured during my time with this man. My innocent former self died that year. I was nine.

I was sixteen years old and in therapy for several suicide attempts when my therapist discovered the sexual abuse. It was at this time my parents were made aware of what happened. I am not sure if his wife knew of his actions at the time because they had since divorced. No charges were filed. My abuser has since passed away and can no longer hurt anyone. I will admit, when I heard of his death I felt like I could breathe again. I did not see Frank after I turned twelve and my family moved to Pennsylvania. I would never be able to confront him or tell him how much he hurt me and changed the outcome of my life.

People can rationalize situations they read about. However, when you are in the direct center of a situation, it's not as easy as you might think. I was already petrified of being taken away from my home, because having to stay with other people had become such a routine occurrence. I did not want to take any chances of losing my family. My greatest fear was that I'd be forced to live with this man forever. I felt I had to walk a very fine line.

During the months I spent going back and forth, between my house and his, I grew up faster than any child should have to. I learned how to hide things and how to keep secrets. I would make believe that I was another child living in completely different circumstances. I pretended mother's illness was my illness and her problems were my problems. I didn't give myself time to internalize the physical and emotional torture I was enduring. By creating a life that was not really mine, I found a way to escape from all the pain. I just wanted to be the person God would have made me if everything had not gone so wrong.

I lost whatever happiness I had along with any trust I had for people and the world. Trust did not exist. Once my mother became ill, bad feelings took over any good that were left. There was never time to deal with the emotions that arose from my sexual abuse. Even when I was back home, the emotional chaos continued, and my pain was pushed away in order to deal with the unstable condition of my family life.

The older I got, the angrier I became. I would ask myself the same questions every day. Why wouldn't anyone stop this from happening? Why could they not see the signs of abuse? Why did this have to happen to me? With each unanswered question, I built a new layer of armor around myself. This would keep me protected, but it would also keep everyone out and away from me. Since I no longer trusted anyone, I found hatred comforting. Resentment consumed me.

Sometimes people do not understand us. They overlook us and don't give their support. There may be times when you are ignored or even abused. You might become disappointed. Sometimes, we need to separate from people who no longer nurture us. This is not always easy and many will not understand. We may need guidance and outside support in order to carry this out. Each one of us has the right to choose which people we will spend time with. Not one person can bully you or persuade you once you have set this boundary. You will defend it yourself when you believe in your heart that it will set you free.

After two years of this hellish existence, my parents reconciled and we eventually moved to Pennsylvania. Entering the seventh grade in yet another new school was hard. The prepubescent years are always challenging, to say the least. For me, this time period was a nightmare. Coming to a new town carrying emotional baggage and a dysfunctional home life with me, I didn't stand a chance in hell to make it through the first year.

Looking back, I can see that my experience would have been much different if I had been different. I had no confidence or drive to be a part of any social network or become a member of the "in crowd." Walking through the halls at school, I felt lonely and invisible. I always felt weird and out of place. When I made a few attempts at making friends and took a leap of faith with the popular crowd, I quickly learned that I really did not fit in at all. This did not help my sense of self-worth.

I had no idea how to be "normal" and fit in.

At the time, my definition of normal was to be laughing, smiling, and happy all the time. It included going out to eat with your parents at a restaurant or having them take you and your friends to a shopping mall. Normal people went on family vacations and could be together without domestic disturbance, fighting, screaming and yelling, or constant chaos. I longed for a routine from my parents, with rules and regulations that I must follow, like making sure my homework was completed every night. These were the things I prayed for that others were taking for granted.

I avoided forming friendships in order to keep all of my secrets safe.

As I grew into my early teenage years, things got so much worse. Depression and anxiety consumed my days and nightmares came almost every night. I can remember closing my eyes, holding my breath, and wondering what it would feel like to end my life and no longer exist.

I had no clue how to function around classmates and peers. If I had a sleepover at friend's house, I dreaded going back home. Sometimes, I would stay all weekend, and I'd never get a phone call from my parents inquiring where I was. Imagine the trouble a teenage girl can get herself into when she has no rules or consequences.

I spiraled out of control, doing everything and anything to try and get my mom and dad to notice my existence. If I couldn't gain their attention being good, maybe they'd notice if I was bad, right? Nope! Nothing worked, so I continued to stay on a path of self-destruction, without any form of consequence in sight.

I deliberately surrounded myself with positive people, whether I fit in or not, to get away from the negative atmosphere in my home. But it was impossible to maintain healthy friendships or relationships. I was not capable of feeling that I belonged in any sort of relationship. I felt unworthy of having anything good, so I would destroy everything positive that entered into my life.

I began searching for external things to fill the dark hole in my heart. Good or bad, it never mattered. I tried everything to mask the pain that left me feeling suffocated every day. Nothing worked. I just kept getting angrier. Eventually, I became robotic. I was walking through life numb and without hope, and there was no way out.

I became obsessed with wanting to die. Every minute I was awake, I thought about death. The darkness was still and quiet. There would be no noise, no bad people, no nightmares, and no more pain. My pain was unbearable. My emotions suffocated me until I would hyperventilate and could not catch my breath. I woke up many nights covered in sweat, sitting upright and holding my knees to my chest, rocking back and forth. I would sing or hum quietly to soothe and calm myself. It might take hours to come out of the nightmare and back into the present moment.

I tried to allow my mind to drift into my hopes of how life would one day be. There would be white fences around perfect houses, with kids playing outside. There would be porches with swings, and my mom inside at the stove and dad on a lounge chair, reading the paper. I would take myself to this imaginary place to find peace after all the nightmares.

We should never feel the need to minimize our pain, confusion, or fear. Our situations are real. Your thoughts are real and powerful. They can either be the chains that confine you to your current situation or they can set you free. Sadly, I was stuck and powerless as a child.

During my high school years, I hid my real life, my home life, and who my parents really were. All I ever wanted were "normal" parents who didn't fight, who weren't sick, and who didn't do drugs. I wanted parents I could count on.

I began smoking in my early teens and by then, my addiction to sugar was out of control. Coming off sugar addiction is just as bad as any other drug. Sugar does damage and takes a toll on one's emotional well-being. Your mood can be altered and your energy levels will spike and then crash. You eventually begin to feel like crap! I used to sit down and eat two boxes of donuts, a bag of chocolate candy, cupcakes, cookies, ice cream, anything to satisfy my cravings. The amount of sugar I was consuming each day should have put my body into sugar shock. It was ridiculous how much sugar I could eat.

I continued searching in all the wrong places for affection, for love, for anyone and anything to fill this emptiness. I longed for emotional attachment and security from anyone. I was starving for something, but I could not put my finger on it—so I would just eat and eat. People who overeat must get to the root of why we binge and consume enormous amounts of calories.

Every client I have worked with who suffers from an eating disorder has eventually discovered that the problem was never about the food itself or being hungry. Something needs attention. Eating disorders are a form of personal abuse. Some may not be aware at the time, but eventually they come to realize it was always something inside of them that happened or that needed attention.

When I interview an overweight client, nine times out of ten, I find that they are eating when they are not hungry. They eat when they are happy, sad, active, or still. They will eat all the time. Then there are the clients who will never admit to their calorie consumption in the beginning, but by the end, the outcome is the same. They were embarrassed to admit their caloric intake to themselves, let alone to me.

Anorexia and Bulimia Nervosa don't lead to obesity, but they are also conditions in which a person abuses himself or herself by starving, throwing up, or using laxatives. Previous clients have expressed their need to control their lives through these behaviors. Therapy revealed the reason was because they felt they had absolutely no control over a bad situation. Eating disorders should all be taken seriously.

Working with clients over the past decade has taught me to be honest with them about dysfunctional eating. They are not alone, and the struggle is real. I use the knowledge I gained from my personal experience and give them resources where they can find help. They must be willing to get to the root cause in order to change their self-destructive behaviors.

Overeating gave me a temporary state of euphoria, excitement, and happiness. I felt in control of something for the first time in my life. Food gave me power and comfort! Food was my safe place. However, immediately following the act of binge eating six thousand calories (or sometimes more), I felt worse. I hated myself and the behavior. I prayed to wake up and be anyone else but me. I was trapped in a body I did not respect, and I felt my mind that was not strong enough to stop the self-abusive behavior.

I also searched for male attention. Good or bad, it didn't matter; anything would do. Being in a relationship gave me an outlet for my rage and aggression. Most of my boyfriends suffered the wrath of my downward spiral to what I call HELL. My life felt like a living hell. I tested each relationship with my disruptive behaviors, crazy antics, and need to control. I was consumed with jealousy and hatred if they showed love, affection, or attention to anyone but me. The jealousy got so bad, I found myself raging, screaming, and fighting with my boyfriends over everything. All of the relationships would eventually come to an end. My reputation for being "crazy" grew as I got older.

We are all products of our environments. What we are taught and what we learn as children becomes how we respond to society and how we treat others. Growing up, I was taught you had to fight in all of your relationships. Things were "normal" when there was chaos, sadness, and disruptive behaviors. I never saw consequences for bad behaviors, so why would I strive for greatness? Everything I hated about my childhood, I had become. How could I despise something so much, but then live the same way?

I will never forget how, at the age of sixteen, I would have my boyfriend drop me off after a date at a house that was not really mine. I lied about where I lived because I didn't want him to see my parents or the unstable environment I was living in.

It wasn't the physical appearance of our house that bothered me, because the house itself was beautiful. My father had built the log cabin we lived in. It was my mother's dream home, and he always tried to deliver on her expectations. He worked full time during the day and then devoted long hours at night building our home. This house was nestled in the woods in a beautiful location.

But I wanted to hide what was living inside the house and the sadness thriving in the walls and every brick of the foundation. I did not want to expose the raw and ugly truth of my family to anyone.

Eventually, my boyfriend discovered I was lying—so of course, I had to tell another lie to cover my embarrassment. How do you explain a situation that you yourself do not understand? How does a sixteen-year-old explain all the darkness and crazy circumstances of her home life? I couldn't. I lied to cover up what I didn't want revealed.

I became a professional liar at a very young age. I was able to disguise the truth, and I became very good at telling stories to keep others from uncovering my reality. But we lived in a small town where everyone knows everyone and nothing gets past people. Other parents knew who my parents were and what they were doing. They would try to keep their children away from me in order to keep them safe. The town knew about the drugs, though I didn't know they knew. Many of my mother's extracurricular activities were the talk of the town.

So there I was, telling stories and lies, when everyone knew the truth. Talk about embarrassment and shame! The reality of my life made its way through every household until every classmate, family member, and friend knew what was going on. My life was exposed, and once again, neither of my parents showed an ounce of remorse or compassion. They made no attempt to rectify the situation. Everyone just continued to live the way they wanted, without a care in the world about how much this hurt me. You can't imagine how hard it was to face my peers, to walk down the halls and be called every name in the book. I had no one with whom I was safe.

My attempts at creating a make-believe life were always short-lived. The truth will come out. Now, I look at that as a good thing. Lying and pretending were exhausting. I always forgot the story of my first lie, and then had to tell another lie to cover up my forgetfulness, and the pattern continued. It was an endless cycle of dishonesty.

Habits are formed by repetition. If you do something all the time, it will become a habit. This can either benefit your current life and situation, or it can lead to failure and disappointment.

All I wanted was a new start. I needed to brush off my family's reputation and move forward with conscious effort into a life that had no room for lies. However, that did not happen.

I spent my teenage years covering up the truth and my real life. The full spectrum of dysfunctional events that went on inside of my home were not revealed until I was in my late thirties, but the town knew enough to make me feel like an outcast.

Being a teenager is HARD. You are picked on and pressured every day unless you fall into a certain status. I was made fun of throughout my high school years for many reasons. One thing I will never forget is how it felt to walk down the halls hearing whispers and negative comments about how chubby I was or what I had done at a party over the weekend. The sadness and depression got so bad that all I wanted to do was die. I felt no reason to live. My home life was awful, and school was worse. I felt alone and scared with no one to turn to. I dreamed about dying.

The way we feel during a certain moment is not a good way to judge what is actually going on in our lives. The current situation never stays. You have to search for inner strength and look ahead to every possibility, knowing that things won't always be bad. I understand now that nothing and no one is worth death. This life is worth living, and you are worth every breath.

As a teen, I was incapable of holding onto anything good. I was pretty much winging life, teaching myself every important component to self-care, love, and acceptance. When something good happened, I destroyed it. I sabotaged all good things that came my way because, to be honest, I didn't like or respect myself—so why even try?

I hated who I was and hated what happened to me. I hated the life I was given. With each new mistake came a new form of self-hate. I felt stuck in a miserable life with no end in sight.

Looking back to how I felt at those exact moments of despair, I realize there is always something bigger than our current situation. There are always more important events waiting for us. We are much bigger than our past mistakes. When you feel stuck, hold on to all hope. We all have been placed on this earth for a reason. Don't ever give up on a better life.

When I was sixteen, my parents finally divorced. I begged to move back to Florida to live with my grandmother. And so, for my senior year, I left the mess behind and began a new life. I would be free from all the nightmares, sadness, and dark days. Free from all the mistakes. Up until this point, I had moved from Florida to Delaware, back to Florida, and to Pennsylvania. Now I'd be finishing high school in Winter Haven, the place I was born, where I hoped to find peace and freedom.

Moving in with my grandmother saved my life. I'd already survived three suicide attempts. I had felt there was no other way to escape the unbearable pain in my heart, and I knew that no matter what I did, the wounds grew deeper. I was still so lost.

With this return to Florida, the scenery changed and the fighting stopped. I no longer went to bed hearing screaming and yelling in the house. Grandma's house seemed pretty peaceful. My living environment changed for the better.

My grandmother and I bonded and spent time together. This was what I had been craving for so many years. I loved the house I was living in, and I loved and respected her and everything she stood for. Our Friday night traditions consisted of watching movies and eating cheesecake. Her home was a wonderful place filled with many happy memories.

Yet why was I still so angry? I was far away from what had hurt me, but I continued screwing up. How did I get so crazy and become so out of control? It seemed like everything I touched fell apart.

My senior year was one of the best years I had during high school. No one knew my past, and I NEVER exposed the truth to anyone—including my boyfriend at the time. But even though I verbalized a fairytale childhood, my actions told a completely different story. People could see my emotional pain, and some soon discovered things were not as I had explained.

Then parents were talking and kids were talking, and my situation was once again exposed. The past I had created was just a fantasy.

Classmates began to question my authenticity and intentions. My motives had never been to harm anyone. I had just wanted to protect myself from being abandoned and rejected, judged and ridiculed, or worse—simply forgotten.

I continued with my childlike antics and disruptive outbursts. I gave my opinion and fought with everyone, even the ones who had no desire to fight back. Fighting made me feel better. I was able to vent, scream, and yell until I was too exhausted to continue. It seemed I was always angry at someone. I screamed and yelled at my "friends," boyfriends, and family members, usually for no reason. I was just pissed off all the time. I found fault in everyone and everything. I was angry at the world and everyone who lived it.

It's important to be free to show how you feel. To be "real" means to be honest about our emotions. Don't discourage your tears any more than you discourage the laughter. There will be times throughout your life you will need to express both.

My food addiction was so bad by the end of high school that I gained almost twenty pounds that year. My cravings for sugar and fats were out of control. I could not get a handle on my portion sizes, and to be honest, I didn't care to. I was consumed with guilt and regret, all while sabotaging my body. My food abuse gave me comfort and covered up what was really going on in my heart.

My boyfriend was a handsome young man who was adored by many women. All heads would turn when he walked down the halls in school. I could never stop looking at him because of his external beauty. We had met at the complex where I was babysitting.

Soon after we started dating, I became consumed with jealousy of anyone he talked to. I realize now that my jealousy stems from a fear of abandonment. I was always afraid he would find someone better and leave me. It became an obsession. I smothered him so much, he ended up leaving. I don't blame him one bit, looking back on my actions. At the time, I felt I needed to control his every thought and move in order to keep him from leaving.

Any relationship I was involved in seemed to make things worse for me. Instead of finding comfort from others and bonding more than just physically, I would find myself angry, lost, and afraid. I was terrified that they would leave me. I did not know how to react to any form of physical and emotional relations. Most people find companionship to be gratifying. I was the exact opposite.

I went from choking down three cigarettes a day to smoking two packs a day. I loved the way nicotine made me feel. I loved that I could use it to replace food. I dropped twenty-five pounds in the first few months—although that weight eventually found its way back, because my food addiction was not gone. I now was addicted to food *and* nicotine. Talk about anxiety! The negative effects that all those chemicals had on my body left me feeling awful!

# CHAPTER TWO

# ARMOR OF LIES

If you're unhappy, your discontent is not something you should ignore or stuff down in shame or with food. Rather, it's something to face head on. You have to work to change. Sometimes, changing means leaving—a situation, a group, or even a place.

Not everyone will understand your decision to leave, and that's okay. You don't need a group consensus. You just need to trust your truest truth. Some people will cheer you on and others will beg you to stay. But at the end of the day, your choices belong to you.

My only comfort came only in the form of food, eating, and nicotine. I was eating enormous amounts of food. I ate so much, I would become physically sick. And then one day, a high school friend introduced me to anorexia. Well, I quickly found out I was not able to starve myself, because I loved food way too much. But I tried binge eating and then trying to throw up.

It wasn't as easy as I thought it would be. I was not able to make myself vomit. Trust me, I tried so hard that I injured the back of my throat with a toothbrush—but I still had no luck. I just couldn't do it.

Then I discovered laxatives. In my mind, I tried to justify this by telling myself this would be so much better than throwing up. Laxatives soon became my go-to "drug" of choice. I would stop at three or four fast-food restaurants after work then take a half of a box of laxatives. It felt disgusting—and my weight stayed the same! I may have lost a few pounds, but I did not get the results I had hoped for. In fact, I eventually started to gain weight, despite all of the laxatives I was taking.

This behavior continued for many years after high school. It got to the point I was taking up to six boxes of laxatives a week. Eventually, that caught up to me, big time. My sister and I were vacationing in Venezuela when I started noticing there was a thick layer of bloody white mucus when I would have a bowel movement. I was also experiencing abdominal cramps, but I assumed they were hunger pains and disregarded them. By the time we got back to the U.S., my symptoms had become severe. Every time I went to the bathroom, I felt excruciating pain, and there was always blood. I had no choice but to stop taking laxatives and go to the doctor. By the time my appointment day arrived, I was doubled over in pain.

After running multiple tests, the doctors discovered I had done permanent damage to my digestive track by consuming such large amounts of laxatives. I had torn the lining in my rectum and had numerous stomach ulcers that would never fully heal.

I went back and forth in my mind, trying to find ways to justify taking just a few laxatives a week—but each time I did, the terrible pain would return. It actually took me a few months, but I finally was able to stop. Thank God I did, because the damage I had already done was extensive. I can't imagine what would have happened had I continued.

After graduating from Winter Haven High School, I enlisted in the United States Navy. I did not do it out of any sense of patriotism. I did it because I felt that it would help earn points and validation from my family. I thought I might finally do something they could be proud of me for. They did seem proud and supportive of my decision to enlist.

But once I got to boot camp, I hated it. I surely did not like the rules, structure, and schedules, and being away from everyone I knew frightened me. I was lonely and afraid. I didn't know what it was at the time, but I suffered from separation anxiety. It would take many years before I understood this part of myself. Until I did, it really ran me around.

Throughout boot camp, my food consumption was out of control. Enlisting in the Navy did not produce the results I had hoped for. I'd expected to turn into a strong woman defending our country with pride and dignity, holding a level of respect for myself and enjoying how others viewed me. Sadly, this was not the outcome.

Instead, I became more and more addicted to food. I would wake up at all times of the night to eat, and at mealtime, my portions were insanely large. My depression got much worse as I got bigger, but I could not stop eating. Because of all of the new sadness I was feeling, I slipped into a deep, dark, food-driven depression that left me drained and exhausted.

During one of my phone calls home, I discovered my mother had had another relapse. For me, that was a blessing in disguise, because I was able to leverage it into an honorable discharge from the military to care for my mother. After receiving the discharge, I flew home to face my dysfunction.

Although my mother's illness had been my ticket out of a bad situation, I felt like a failure. I had not been willing or able to adapt to the physical and mental demands required to be a strong soldier. I left the service weaker than I had been before enlisting. I felt broken.

I had gained so much weight that many of my high school friends didn't believe I'd been in the Navy. They thought it was all a lie, even though two of them had driven me to the airport and watched me leave! Could I blame them? I'd been away so briefly and I came home before I could even graduate from military boot camp. I even contacted one of our high school classmates who I had run into in the galley one day at boot camp and asked her to verify that I had really been there. But eventually, I stopped trying to convince others and chalked it up to a learning experience.

I moved back in with my mother for a short time. It was not a healthy environment. She was worse than I remembered. My parents were divorced, but lived within twenty minutes of each other. I shuffled between their houses, but that was miserable. Eventually, I moved to Pittsburgh with a few classmates from high school.

That was one of the darkest times in my life. I was so lost and confused, and my life had no purpose. I was going through the motions, numb and without goals, living one day at a time without any clue as to where I was going. Food continued to be my source of comfort. I tried alcohol, but I hated the taste, so I didn't get involved with that. I tried pot and was not impressed, so that was the extent of my experimenting with street drugs. Besides, I was scared to death of all the others, because I had seen my parents' response to being high throughout my childhood. I refused to allow myself to touch drugs.

When I was nineteen, I was at a party one night and I witnessed some of the people there doing hard drugs. As we sat around a small table, playing cards, one of the men pulled out a bag and a piece of aluminum foil. Wrapped inside was a white powder and glass pipe. He began to prepare a translucent, hard ball. When he lit it, the smell was awful. I can remember asking my friend what in the heck he was smoking. It was crack cocaine

The party hosts were in their forties or older. I can remember running out of the house and tearing down the street. I literally ran all the way to a place I felt was safe enough to stop and call a cab. I was scared to death they would come after me. I knew in that moment that I would never touch any sort of drug, ever!

People who take drugs are frightening. They turn into unfamiliar beings and have out-of-body experiences, unaware of their surroundings. They're oblivious to how their actions can destroy all who are around them. I always thought succumbing to drugs was a selfish act until I came to understand why people make this choice. Many times, they have lost all control over their situation. Their drug of choice consumes their thought process. They live to be high and are unable to stop without assistance and guidance from professionals trained to help people detox in a safe way.

I have great empathy for those who have gone down this path, because I know that if they were able to stay sober long enough to get help, they could uncover the underlying cause of their addictions. Not one of us has a right to judge anyone. What we don't understand leaves us uneducated and clueless. We must learn to live with compassion and understand that it is not in our human nature to try to mess up our lives. Most of us are taught, in a variety of ways, how to survive in this world. If you find yourself in a situation where you feel it's your business to judge, pause and take a moment to understand the circumstances first.

I thank God every day for giving me the courage to walk away from drugs. Looking back on that situation at the party, my life could have turned out so differently. What if I had taken one hit of crack cocaine or injected one syringe of heroin? I know that, with my addictive personality, I might have turned to hard drugs to satisfy my needs. Thank you, God, for giving me a guardian angel that night, and for giving me the strength and courage to get up and to run away that night in Pittsburgh.

When we finally take responsibility for our own happiness, we find we are assuming a very big responsibility.

I eventually went back to Bloomsburg, Pennsylvania, and moved in with my father. While bartending in a local restaurant there, I met the man who would become my first husband. At first, I was not interested in "Joe" (not his real name), but eventually, I began to look forward to seeing him when he stopped in the bar on his way home from work. We started dating, and before too long, he introduced me to his mother and father.

His mom was kind and exuded so much love for her son that I was in awe over it. Their relationship was sweet and loving. It was comforting to watch. I enjoyed being in the presence of such kindness. I had not experienced anything quite like it before, and I was instinctively drawn to it. I remember thinking, if Joe and I married one day, she would be my mother. It was my dream to have a mother like her. She loved her children so much and she was full of life, energy, and good vibes. I believed that marrying this man would give me a life I had always dreamed of having.

He and I spent a lot of time with his family, who I grew to be very comfortable with. Being in the presence of such positive love was new to me. It was a breath of fresh air to experience this form of joy, comfort, and contentment. I learned many things from his mother, including the basics I had never learned from my own mother, like how to clean and cook. I had an enormous amount of respect and love for this woman, and I was so thankful for all she taught me.

I don't really think she knew how much she was helping to make me a better person by being a positive influence in my life at this time. I watched her with her children and husband and I began to mimic her behavior, trying to do things the way she did. I loved what she stood for—she was inspiring!

"Joe" and I got engaged, I became pregnant, and we got married. Things between my mom and I were the best they ever were during that period. Being pregnant with my first daughter brought my mother and me to a new level of closeness. We were spending time together and doing things mothers and daughters do. She was in a good place at the time, too. I believe she was looking forward to meeting her grandchild and I thought it would give her a second chance at parenting. She never said that to me, but that was my impression based on how she acted during my pregnancy.

I was visiting my mother almost every day. She would have lunch or dinner made for us and she went out of her way to help us throughout my pregnancy. I felt a bond with her during this time, and I embraced every moment I spent with her. I hold this memory very close to my heart. I will cherish these memories forever.

When my daughter was born, I watched my mother expressing so much love and joy around her. That gave me the opportunity to see my mother in a whole new way. I developed a level of respect for her and I enjoyed the relationship the three of us were building.

I slowly licked my childhood wounds and embraced this new relationship. I began to forgive her for the things she had done wrong while I grew up.

The birth of my daughter awakened a sense of effortless and unconditional love in me—my need to protect her from all things that could potentially harm her. I felt so much love for this child, even before she born. She was my princess, my own little miracle. She was my beautiful creation. I was so taken with her that I began forming obsessive-compulsive behaviors and going to the extreme in many ways that were not healthy.

I felt the need to be perfect, look perfect, and have the perfect home for my daughter to live in. I spent hours every day disinfecting our house, cleaning, organizing, and rearranging things so they appeared to be perfect. My husband built a house that could be considered the home of my dreams. It was beautiful, big, and white with a perfectly manicured landscape and lawn.

My obsessive needs were getting much worse around the time we moved into our home. I was cleaning all the time. I never welcomed anyone into my home because I didn't want them to disturb the order I had created. When people did come over, I made them go through a process before entering the house. They had to take off their shoes and wash their hands. When I came home, I immediately showered and changed the clothes I was wearing so I could avoid contaminating the house with germs. This became a serious issue for many years.

Now, here is the strange part of this: my house, my car, and my physical appearance seemed perfect. But if you opened a drawer, closet, or pantry, you would find they were a disaster. The funny thing about this, as I look back on the situation, is this was exactly how was feeling. My appearances had to be perfect, but my mind and emotional self were a mess. I felt dirty and disgusting, therefore I would clean. Over the years, I would struggle with this again and again—but once I was able to "spring clean" my mind, the strong desire for personal perfection would become obsolete.

# CHAPTER THREE

# WE MEET AGAIN

My happiness was short-lived. The dark memories prevailed, and I began searching for ways to sabotage my current life. I felt I was not worthy of anything good.

More specifically, I believed I was not worthy of the people who were good to me and loved me. My comfort was not in happiness, it was in pain and misery. I found my contentment in negative emotions because pain and suffering, chaos and uncertainty were the only things I had ever known.

I began acting out again, looking for anything to mask the dark hole in my heart. I lived with an uncontrollable fear that, at any given moment, I could lose my family. This feeling would not subside.

I became unattached and emotionally separated from those I loved most, and the downward spiral began again. I remember holding my daughter and praying that I would get better. I needed to do something to make this baby girl proud of her mama! She was the only thing at that time in my life that I worked for. I was always protecting her from everything and anything.

People would tell me I needed to loosen up with her as she got older, but I was too afraid. What if something happened to her? What if someone hurt her? This little human was my world, and I lived only to be her mother.

As everything around me began to fall apart, I was unable to hide the emotional trauma. It forced its way back to the surface. I was no longer able to control my feelings by eating. So I tried a new route: diet pills. This was it! *This* would save me—or so I thought.

As I wiped my tears away, I called my husband and said, "I want to be a nurse." He was skeptical, but eventually he came around. I applied and was accepted into the 1998 Penn College nursing program. This was my way of doing something to help the world, giving a piece of myself that would be beneficial to society. I felt my daughter would respect me as a nurse. It also was the career my mother-in-law at the time had chosen. I was going to make something out of all the bad things that had happened in my life.

At first, nursing school went well. My grade point average was 3.9-4.0. I discovered, through my studies, that my Obsessive Compulsive Disorder was contributing to every aspect of my studies. I felt I had to ace every test, nail every lab, and get 100 percent on each clinical. I would not accept failure or a bad score on a test.

Juggling a part-time job, a husband, and a toddler—while going to school full-time—was much harder than I'd anticipated. It was exhausting. But I continued to strive for perfection in all areas of my life: school, appearance, motherhood, you name it, I had to be the best in all the external factors in my life.

Inside, however, I was falling apart. I couldn't maintain a workable study schedule. When I scored a 72 on one of my lab tests, I finally realized I needed to do something. I discovered the energy enhancement/weight loss drugs called Thermolift and MetaboLife. They were my lifesavers during these college years. I was able to stay awake all night to study and still have energy to play with my daughter. The best part was, I was dropping weight! I lost more than fifty pounds in a very short time.

Of course, I was irritable and cranky. My temper was exploding all the time, but I did not make the connection between that and the legal drugs I was taking. The demands of school and my lack of sleep were causing me to be perpetually on edge.

While fully legal at the time, this drug has since been pulled from all the shelves. These energy enhancements were found to cause many health issues, such as heart attacks, in addition to anxiety and depression. Wait! Was this the cause of my downward spiral into an anxiety-driven depression? Could it be possible this drug was making me crazy? A chemical nightmare was going on inside of my body.

I was already high-strung and anxiety-driven by nature. Now I was taking something that would amplify all of these symptoms. After studying the side effects and truly understanding the shift in my mood and actions, I slowly stopped taking all of the pills. I could not sleep, could not eat, and my OCD was out of control.

I had a breakdown and had to quit school while I detoxed from all of the pills I had been taking to try to manage my life. I ended up needing to take an anti-anxiety drug to help calm my craziness and off-the-wall behaviors that I had developed from taking those pills.

I failed. I quit school. I did not accomplish what I'd set out to do with my education. As a result, failure became my new habit over the next few years. Everything I touched fell apart.

My second daughter was born as I was reaching the lowest point in my life. She was another little miracle, a blessing who entered this world bringing her unique personality, love, and innocence. She was one of the most beautiful babies in the world and one of the sweetest. She was so easy to take care of. Her personality and funny disposition made me laugh and feel pride, even in the midst of my self-judgment and depression. This little human was going to do amazing things in her lifetime. She was one of the greatest gifts God had given me.

Learning how to be a good mother was a real challenge because of the mindset I had developed. I tried so hard to parent perfectly and shelter my children from the world. I thought I was doing a good thing for them by protecting them from harm, when I was actually preventing them from building confidence. I am sure all of you have heard the term "if I could have done things differently." I look back on how I tried to shelter my children without understanding I was really holding them back. I wish I could have known then what I know now, but life does not work that way. We must learn from all of our past mistakes and make choices to change them. I know I did everything out of commitment and love for them, but I could have done things so much better!

The unconditional love I felt for my children was effortless. I might test and even sabotage my own life, but when it came to them, I tried to hide all my faults and imperfections. Wow, was I wrong in thinking this way. It is okay to show our children we are imperfect and human. We will make mistakes, just like they will, and we will sometimes do things we are not proud of.

Let your children know it is perfectly fine to mess up. They are going to make mistakes, and seeing that you can, too, will help them to realize they are not alone and their behaviors are a part of growing up and learning. That's what life is all about. Had I been the person back then that I am today, their lives could have been so different. But here is the thing: you can't go back and change anything. What you can do is take action and create the skills you wish you had applied to your parenting in previous years. Have the courage to accept what was and change what will be.

What your heart yearns for is not just a personal desire. It is your calling. Be sure to listen and answer the call.

I was divorced with two children by age twenty-six. Things tend to get worse before they get better. I tried, tested fate, and slipped into another anxiety-driven depression.

The thing is, I did not wake up saying, "I really hope I mess up today!" I tried so hard, with what little knowledge I had, to be "normal." I tried to not act out and to feel love and happiness. I just could not. This would go on for many years.

"Like a sword with two edges, your words can create the most beautiful dream, or they can destroy everything around you." Forgiveness is the only way to heal. Self-forgiveness can be the hardest of all.

CHAPTER FOUR

# A FAMILY GROWS

"Flaws" are just projected fears ... I used to create fear by comparing myself to others. I have learned that if we feel internally imprisoned, no amount of money or outside praise will ever make us feel free. The path to freedom is to get rid of the things or people that no longer matter, and then share your story and your true self. Happiness and success thrive within us and how we perceive ourselves.

As you can clearly see, I have not always been happy—in fact, I have spent many years in deep struggle. Fulfillment and happiness are achieved by self-love, not by any one external factor like a relationship or career choice. In order to find happiness, you must look first within. Isn't it interesting how much we have to work at being happy sometimes?

I have worked hard to get to the happiness at this stage in life. I have made so many bad decisions. I have also made many very good decisions, including some that did *not* feel good at the time and that were not easy. I made those decisions because I knew they were the right thing to do. Sometimes it took me years to integrate and heal. I prayed for unconditional trust, not only in myself, but in others.

In my early childhood years, I had learned to mistrust the world and all the people in it. When something tragic happens to you as a child, it influences your outlook as an adult. But the road you choose to live as an adult is *your* responsibility and yours alone!

Throughout my life, I followed my intuition, no matter what it told me or how weird it seemed. Sometimes it has been confusing to my mind, but I have chosen to listen to my gut. People have misunderstood me, questioned me, and judged me. It used to really hurt my feelings. Now, I have no apologies for the person I am, my choices, my intuition, or my values. I stand behind them 100 percent. I am free and liberated.

I have also spent many years reprogramming my DNA, rewiring from scarcity to prosperity and consciousness. I am committed to my journey, and grace has met me in the process. I will not allow my past to define my true self. I am so grateful for this day—so grateful for this happiness, and so grateful for my life and for all of the beautiful people I am able to inspire with my true story. My passion is simply to make others' lives better.

It is funny how we tend to think a small step is not really that effective. We will use every excuse in the book to stand still and not move. The awesome reality is, all of the small steps you are taking will make the best and biggest changes.

Despite my struggles and failure with nursing school—or maybe because of them—at some point I got sick and tired of being sick and tired. I began awakening to the idea that it was time for me to grow and transform by allowing changes that were necessary.

I had spent most of my life holding back and not allowing natural changes to occur that might have helped me grow and heal from previous tragic events. My hesitancy had affected many years of my life.

Even so, I eventually met my current husband, the love of my life, the man who would teach me more than I could ever imagine. I began to proceed without doubt and hesitation. I would carry regrets, but I moved forward, embracing my relationship with an open heart. Through thick and thin—good, bad, and in-between—this man would show me what a healthy love felt like.

> "We must learn to control the emotions so we have
> enough personal power to change our fear-based agreements,
> escape from hell, and create our own personal heaven."
> —Ruiz

When I first read this quote, I realized how much it resonated with me. Our emotions are the trapped energies and old feelings we hold close to our hearts. When they surface throughout the day, we become trapped, and we repeat our same, unwanted patterns. There will come a time in all of our lives when we decide to take back our personal peace and power and create a fresh, new lifestyle.

I moved into this relationship with an unbelievable sense that this man was *the one*. I can't explain the connection he and I had, but it was honest-to-goodness real! This relationship was so much different than the others had been. Something inside of me was screaming to make peace with my past in order to open up to this man, who offered a genuine love—not only for me, but for all of my baggage, too.

We will be married thirteen years in October. Our relationship has been through just about everything a marriage can possibly go through. We have built our marriage out of pure love and a foundation of trust that is stronger and more binding than anything I can think of. We have had our share of ups and downs, disappointments, and struggles along the way. But we always end up with a resolution and a stronger bond because of all of the challenges we have faced.

My husband has stood by me through all my tantrums, outbursts, and insecurities. He has fought like hell to help me understand myself and my actions. He has had my back through it all. Before him, I found it challenging to attach to anyone other than my children. I had ended and destroyed all my previous relationships because I did not have the understanding of how to emotionally bond to others.

At the beginning of our relationship, I was no different with this man. I cannot tell you how many times I tried to push him away. So many times, I would slip into a dark place and try to do everything in my power to get him to leave me. But he wouldn't. He never left me. Even during the times he really should have left, he stayed and helped me get past whatever I was going though at the time.

He learned that if he hugged me during a fit of rage, I would immediately calm down. He continued to hug me through some of our toughest moments, even when I was not approachable. His gentle nature and determination to help me break that wall I spent a lifetime building eventually worked. He was able to help get me through some of my worst memories through the simple act of hugging.

I do not know how in the world I became so lucky, but I thank God every day for this beautiful man. With his support and unconditional love, I slowly began to believe in myself. I began to open my wings and allow myself to feel for the first time *ever*! I began to like myself. I gained a little more confidence every day.

Opening myself to his "hugging" therapy put me in a vulnerable situation. I had always been petrified of touching and feelings, because they made me feel weak. I would think to myself, *at any moment this man could leave or hurt me.* But he hasn't left yet, and he has certainly never hurt me. He has been a big factor and turning point on which direction my life would go.

"A ship is safe in harbor, but that's not what ships are for."
—William G.T. Shedd

Eventually, I had gained enough confidence to follow my heart and bring my passion for helping others to the public. We have the right to dream and take the responsibility to do everything we can to make our dreams come true.

With this new confidence and healthy love I had in my life, I became driven and passionate about life and learning. I began researching and taking online courses to educate myself about the health and fitness industry. During nursing school, I had discovered that I was fascinated with the chemistry of the human body and how it worked. I had a love for fitness and a passion to help others.

Nursing school made me realize I would not be a good nurse, because I was not able to stomach all of the germs. I admire people in the medical field. It takes a special person to give themselves freely to helping those who are sick and in need. But I was not cut out for that career.

I began to design and implement healthy programs to help people. They were not quick fixes, but programs that required personal commitment. I stayed up at night and spent all of my free time researching and studying nutrition, fitness, and mental healing. I invested a great deal of time and money keeping myself current on these topics. I continued to receive credits and certifications from a number of respected organizations. You can never have too much knowledge when it comes to your career. Keep yourself up-to-date with all new strategies. Always learn new ways and leave room for improvements.

Not only had my life changed drastically, but my clients were changing their lives with my programs. The health reports they got from their doctors showed positive changes. Doctors were lowering their medications, which was a huge win for many of them. The focus wasn't always weight loss; those non-scale victories also were piling up! My knowledge was helping others in a healthy, positive way.

My passion continued to grow as my fitness family did. I had seemed to figure it out. I had the perfect husband and family. My career was booming, and I was happy.

Then came another life-changing event. I had a miscarriage, which was very sad for my husband and me. It would have been a child we had created together. Life went on, and I made it through, but something seemed wrong. My periods did not resume.

Thinking the worst, I went to the doctor. After checking me, he came up with a surprise diagnosis: I was pregnant! I didn't believe it. I thought the test results were reflecting my body's attempt at recovering from the miscarriage. But he was right. Three years after I began taking off in the fitness world, our son was born.

His arrival was a blessing for sure. I had my two daughters from my first marriage, and my husband had a son from his first marriage. Now we had a child of our own, which brought the total count to four. Our blended family would be united by the birth of this baby.

What did I ever do before kids? They change everything in such a positive way. Children give a whole new meaning to love and contentment. To this day, I know my greatest success is my children. Over the years, we spent all of our free time with the kids, and any extra money we had went into my education and building my career.

After working at a local gym for four years, things in my life spiraled out of control, yet again. This time it was different, and the outcome of the situation would lead to unbelievable and unexpected blessings. What I thought was the end of my existence was really the beginning of a new life and a whole new way of living. I would soon find myself in the midst of uncertainty and chaos—but amazing life surfaces after some of the darkest days.

The situation I had put myself in at the time was toxic and unhealthy. I knew this going in, but I was not able to separate from it in order to save myself. Remember, chaos and havoc were things I found comfort in. This time, all the bad, awful things that were happening to me and to my family were suddenly about to make sense. But before that could happen, things had to get pretty rough.

If you don't live in a small town, then you have only peripheral awareness of what goes on in places like the one we live in. In our town, everyone knows what you are doing at all times, often including when you eat and when you sleep—and with whom. There are positive things about raising your children in a small community, and there are negative aspects as well. Some people thrive off of the mistakes of others and make up things along the way. Before you know it, your life can become everyone's favorite topic of discussion.

Often, in the retelling, a story becomes so twisted that you end up looking very bad. Then suddenly, you're being treated like trash. Heads turn away when you enter a room. People act as if they don't know you, or they talk under their breath about you to the person they're with.

I have been misunderstood most of my adult life for my mistakes. People make assumptions. I have learned that, unless you are directly involved and have a genuine understanding of the circumstances, you should probably mind your own business.

I discovered through this period that the people who judged and threw stones were the ones who were unhappy in their own lives. I came to understand that I was not just a target but a diversion for them. Obsessing about my life and my mistakes gave them a sense of self-worth. People like that thrive off the pain of others because it gives them comfort as they go through their personal disasters. I forgive them.

No one ever looks good trying to make others look bad. Some people, somehow, prospered off of the shame and sadness I was feeling. They found comfort in my tragedies. I blame myself for placing my life in the path of their destructive behavior. I take full responsibility for all my wrongdoings and the hurt I may have caused others. I have a problem with blaming others for something I did wrong. But you see, the situation was so blown up and so many untrue statements and versions were given, I did not have a chance in HELL to ever save my reputation. Or so I thought.

We are all diamonds and no one can break us! It took something very unusual to get me to that awareness. I placed myself in a twisted relationship scandal that would become blown up and made public by the individuals who were involved. The circumstances were taken so out of context in order to preserve their reputations and completely destroy mine. I was willing to accept my part in all of it and own up to the mistakes I made. But every time I turned around, there was more drama. The individuals involved were going to great lengths to destroy my life, my family, my reputation, and my career.

# CHAPTER FIVE

# TRAUMA IS EXHAUSTING

## What is PTSD?

You might be wondering why I am devoting a chapter to PTSD. What could that possibly have to do with me, when I never saw combat outside of the war raging between my parents when I was a child? The fact is, PTSD had everything to do with my life. It might have something to do with yours.

So, here we go. Post-traumatic stress disorder (PTSD) is a set of reactions that can develop after someone has been through a traumatic event. Any event that involves a threat to life or a serious injury has the potential to be traumatic. This includes natural disaster, war, a serious accident, and a physical or sexual assault. Most people will experience at least one of these types of events during their lives.

In PTSD, you think about these traumatic events long after they're over. You can't stop the thoughts and you can't make them disappear.

What I came to learn, however, was that you can stop them from affecting your life.

Anxiety, anger, and depression are three of the main symptoms that develop in people who have experienced trauma. A sound, smell, or vision from the environment can, without warning, can trigger anxiety and panic. We may find ourselves upset and shaken over the memories that haunt us. A memory may rear its ugly head without any warning at all. Nightmares come and remind us of the tragic event that occurred in earlier years. Then we are left to deal with the emotional side effects.

There are many types of PTSD. A person like me, who suffered from childhood trauma, might tend to unintentionally self-destruct as an adult. For most of my life, I could not understand many of my actions. I would have remorse and feel ashamed, but I was not able to stop the behaviors. It wasn't until the age of thirty-nine that I discovered how to get this part of myself under control.

First, I had to seek help and therapy to reveal some of my darkest childhood memories. Second, I had to go through all of the emotions, such as happy, sad, and angry. The hardest part was actually feeling. I had become numb to emotions in order to keep myself from feeling anything. My protective instincts were to build a barricade and keep people at arm's length to avoid getting hurt. I had lived my teenage years and early adult years feeling isolated because of the "armor" I put around myself. You would never catch me crying, because that was a sign of weakness, and I was determined to prove to the world just how strong I was. The stronger I pretended to be, the more I was falling apart inside.

Third, I had to learn self-love, self-respect, and most of all, self-worth. As a child, I was not taught these three important qualities. How can you learn to love others when you do not love yourself?

You are not born to have respect for others. You are taught to respect yourself and others. Your worth is not how much money you have or how big your home is. It's not your social status. Self-worth is feeling empowered to do great things in this world. Self-worth is setting a positive example and being a respected, reputable, and accountable being.

I do not want to be remembered for all the "bad" I have done. I want to be remembered for all the good I have done.

The mind is a powerful tool, and it can play tricks on us. Things that happened to us years ago can feel like they are happening now, in the present moment. When I try to explain who I am by looking at where I came from or where I grew up, I speak with very little logic and I become confused about my identity. My recollections and experiences are a cluster of awful and hurtful memories. In previous years, I learned to create a life that did not exist to anyone but me.

At the age of thirty-nine, I finally got sick enough of ending up back at the same place, time and time again, that I was willing to do something about it. No matter how great and wonderful things might be going for me at any given time, I had a history of screwing them up. I was finally ready to find the answers and take action—even if it meant I had to leave my family for several weeks. It turned out to be five weeks, to be exact.

I had been in therapy before, so I was back in therapy immediately following my latest episode of personal disaster. However, this therapist was much different. In our sessions, she began noticing signs of something that puzzled her. She pursued what she was seeing and gave me a thorough evaluation. After the dreaded psych evaluation, the diagnosis was clear. I was not bipolar, manic, or a sociopath. I had been sure they would tell me I was all of these things, based on my history and patterns of mistakes. But no—the tests revealed that I suffered from PTSD.

Wow, this was not what I had expected! I thought this condition only happened to veterans who had gone to war and witnessed trauma during their time in service. I imagined veterans who had suffered horrible physical abuse and had witnessed slaughter on a daily basis. I came to understand, very quickly, the meaning and the symptoms of PTSD. It can be brought on by any event that is traumatic to a person's life.

My therapist gave me information and resources where I could seek help. By understanding the cause of my problems, she ended up saving my life.

Though we were skeptical, my husband and I researched many treatment centers until we stumbled across one that really stood out: the Malibu Beach Recovery Center in in Malibu, California. They had what I considered some of the best therapists in the country—but they were an addiction treatment center and didn't handle cases like mine. MBR was well-known and had an excellent reputation for helping addicts recover. They targeted the symptoms first before they treated the disease. This is where my therapist believed their expertise would benefit me. They had some of the best doctors in the world working with their patients.

My husband and the therapist who had diagnosed me spoke to the treatment center many times before they finally agreed to accept me. They were willing to work with me and treat my PTSD as well as my addictions to food, sugar, and unhealthy relationships.

This treatment would cost my family more than $50,000. I had exhausted all of my previous avenues of healing, and I always ended up in self-destruction mode in the end. Now I knew I had to do this, and not only for me. I had to find the answers because I wanted to be free from all that was holding me back. No one said this would happen overnight, but something inside of me was screaming, and knew I would get there.

We are not born with everything we need, but we all have the potential to learn, grow, and work towards happiness. Take one step and you are on your way.

This was my first step. It was time I opened up and was honest about the abuse and neglect I had endured as a child. Talk about being scared to death! I would have rather been anywhere than here.

The center is in a beautiful home in Malibu with some of the finest chefs in the world. They provided Yoga three times a day plus beach walks, self-love classes, painting, and the best therapy money could buy. It scared the heck out of me. In the midst of all the beauty and seeming luxury, I fought with all my might to leave. My internal pain was so unbearable, I became physically ill.

"We wake now. As the veil is lifted, you will see things and hear things for what they truly are. Things will appear very different than before. You will hear more and see more. You will know, as you remember, all you have known and all that is. Do not be afraid, you have known all that is. You are not here by chance, you're honoring an agreement you have made under free will. You have work to do. You are more than you realize. You are powerful and good. You are the light, and will now shine bright. Wake those who are ready and help the indigos/star seeds. We have much support throughout, we are many. Your friends and family from before now. Remember, you are the light, you are the light. It is time to wake up now."

—Michael Gleason

The healing process began and I started to address things that were buried incredibly deep. Only something called Somatic Therapy could pull these dark and hurtful memories out of my mind.

Somatic Experiencing Therapy or SE was developed by Dr. Peter Levine. This type of therapy was designed to help a person move forward from the "frozen" images or memories of their traumatic experiences. When a person endures physical or sexual abuse or any traumatic situation, they may fight back or run away and try to escape reality. But the emotional damage is done. Many times, a person is unable to let go of the pain and the negative memories because they are trapped. Learning to be aware of your body sensations and the mental images that come up when your eyes are closed can help release stored emotions in an effective way.

I can remember leaving one of my sessions with such horrible physical pain that I was unable to function. The trauma and bad memories were present, on the surface, alive and awake. I had spent years stuffing my feelings with food and toxic relationships, and now I was working so hard to fill this place of darkness with positive thoughts and behaviors. I had mastered the art of hiding and forgetting, and I'd had no intentions of revisiting that bad place ever again.

However, during therapy, I started remembering every smell, sound, feeling, and action during a time in my life when I knew nothing more than physical pain and emotional suffering. This was a place I had never consciously returned to, and I was not prepared to experience the physical ramifications of stopping by for a few moments each day to dredge up the events, one by one, until we had uncovered them all.

Every gory, embarrassing detail of what had been done to me as a child began to emerge. It felt like reliving the nightmare all over again, but this time being aware of my feelings. I woke up every night covered in sweat and dreaming of the dual tortures of abuse on the one side and neglect on the other. Each therapy session brought out a new part of my life that had been stuffed into a place I had worked so hard to stay away from.

During my stay at MBR, I learned that my childhood had everything to do with things I had been struggling to avoid most of my life. *I* was not bad and awful, but the things I had experienced and witnessed were bad and awful. I was a reflection of all the things that had happened to me as a child, but I was *not* those things. Yet those moments would affect every decision I made as a teenager and an adult. I would never be able to heal until I revealed the abuse and uncovered the pain, one emotion at a time.

I was so consumed with finding the truth that I spent many hours every day journaling the past and remembering every event that took place. I was able to process the events and finally leave them in a place that I no longer needed to visit. I cried so hard during the night that I was unable to breathe, but there were actually tears this time. I felt them. I had cried for years without shedding one tear. Now they were all coming out, and it was a torrent. Going through this was painful in ways I can barely describe. It was a huge turning point in my life, and when it occurred, I felt like I was ready to go home—or at least, I felt like I had done enough and I wanted to get away from the pain.

I remember calling my husband, Jeff, and begging him to let me come back home. I told him that this was excruciating and I could not bear these awful memories for one more day. I said I was doing better and I could not keep digging up the past and going through all the pain that came from those memories. I was content to leave now.

But he believed there was more benefit to be had. As hard as it was for my husband, he had to be firm and give me tough love. He was my safe place, the one I trusted more than anyone else in the world, other than my children. If he had agreed with me, I would leave California and return home. But he did not agree with me.

Jeff had been speaking to my team of doctors on a regular basis, and he assured me this would get better. He asked me to please trust him and trust the team in Malibu. He explained I needed to complete the treatment and that it was not wise to discontinue half way through.

I did trust him, and even though I disagreed at the time, I let my defenses down and stopped fighting the process of healing. I chose to embrace every step required to gain all the benefits of my team's plan for a healthy recovery. I was an emotional wreck from trying to analyze the past and put all the things into perspective. It was exhausting work.

The truth was, what had happened to me in my childhood was very wrong. There was no justification for the actions certain people had subjected me to. I slowly came to recognize that I hadn't deserved those things that happened to me and, maybe more importantly, that they were not my fault. I came to see that I had no reason to be ashamed or embarrassed, because I was a victim of their abuse.

It was finally time for me to realize there was nothing I could do to change what they had done. However, I *was* able to control how I would allow this situation to continue affecting my life and my future. I could choose to live with self-pity and stay in "poor me" mode, or I could create a diversion that might help others and inspire them to get help and take action in their own lives.

I chose me and I chose to live. I chose to be free from the past trauma I had endured. I chose happiness and peace. I chose to love and forgive the people who had caused me harm. Forgiveness is the only way to heal our wounds.

Finally, I was learning how to put the past into perspective. Think about all of the layers that make up the physical form of the onion. As you begin to peel away and reveal the core, your eyes begin to swell and the tears flow naturally. As I began to peel away each of the layers of my past, I began to swell up with emotion and release years of pain and heartache. Crying and tears would flow as a natural reaction to reliving the trauma.

My therapists were magnificent. I held a level of respect for them that I had never afforded anyone before. I continued to remove the layers of heartache, one at a time, and began to decompress all of the pain that came with uncovering those dark memories.

I started practicing forgiveness of others by learning how to forgive myself first. We must be willing to forgive ourselves first, or forgiveness will be intangible. Part of the human experience is making mistakes. Part of our existence is to get up when we fall, brush ourselves off, and move forward.

The human race was not born perfect. I have yet to meet a person without regrets or mistakes. However, when we hold onto guilt and pain, it becomes self-limiting and unnecessary. It can prevent us from forgiving others. I slowly began to let go of the anger and resentment toward everyone who had harmed me. I became aware of every smell and color that triggered a memory of the bad situations that had caused me all of this internal hate and disgust. It was physically and mentally exhausting.

There were mornings when I would wake up so tired and in such physical pain from the previous days of treatment that I could barely get out of bed.

Once I understood and acknowledged my condition, I began to take all necessary steps to "fix" myself. I cleaned up my thoughts by replacing them with happy memories. I learned to divert the pain by expressing my feelings in a positive and productive way. I created a safe place to put all of those dark memories. They no longer served any purpose in my life and they were no longer welcome to disrupt my thoughts and my actions. They were in the past, which I had no control over. When they tried to reappear, I would quietly place them back into their resting place.

The mind and our thoughts are so powerful that we become what we think. If you think you are bad, you do bad things. If you know your worth and hold yourself to the highest of standards, you develop human morals. Morals are our stepping stones to making good choices and engaging in positive behaviors.

I continued to reveal all of the layers required to get the heart of my self-sabotaging behaviors. I dredged up awareness of the icky details of the deceitful behavior of others, including the adults I had looked up to and trusted, that created in me such feelings of despair. There was no bypassing any of the sordid details. I needed to open each layer and remove the feelings, one by one.

As I moved forward and continued taking steps necessary to letting go of all the hate and anger I felt for those who hurt me, I began to implement the Twelve Steps from the Big Book of AA to help recover from my trauma. Even though I was never an alcoholic, my addictions were just as life-threatening. The Twelve Steps helped me uncover the last several layers of who I really was.

It was through this that I discovered my spiritual path. I learned that my higher power would be something I would turn to on a daily basis. I found an internal place where there were consequences for my actions. I began to feel remorse for all of my bad choices—and then I found a better understanding of those choices.

I realized that I never woke up thinking to myself, "I really hope I can mess up a few people and their lives today." Through honest examination of myself, I began to accept that I had never intentionally set out to cause others pain—even though, somehow, I always did.

As I implemented each of the Twelve Steps, I began to open the door to freedom. The nightmares became less frequent. I found myself walking through a thought process before making any decisions. It felt extraordinary to finally understand consequences and realize something was looking over me all the time.

I loved this connection. It was an amazing feeling to write down previous experiences, take ownership of all of my mistakes, and be completely honest with myself. This process did not happen overnight, or in a few weeks; it took months and became a part of my daily practice, so it was ongoing. Just like anything else in life, recovery would not come without hard work and dedication on my part.

As I moved through each of the Twelve Steps, I felt a sense of physical and emotional relief and personal contentment. I gained confidence. I felt hopeful that there were possibilities everywhere. I was feeling everything, good and bad. When I started the first step, I will admit, I was an emotional wreck. Every bad thing I had ever done, everyone I had hurt, was right there in front of my face, staring at me! Writing out my wrongdoings and then reading them aloud was often unbearable. I found myself asking, how I could have done *that*? Reality hit hard. I had to own up to *all* of my poor decisions, every single one of them. Fortunately, I found that understanding would follow after the completion of each of the steps.

I can remember one specific situation that I easily could have avoided. However, I had craved failure and disappointment, because it had been in my nature to disappoint others. I lived to feel pain and found comfort in being in the midst of chaos. Once I shifted my thinking into a more positive direction and searched for all of the good that came from the bad, I uncovered many disguised blessings.

For all the times I messed up, the hidden lesson would be revealed. I taught myself how to survive in a world where I believed things are not all pretty roses and perfectly painted scenes. I fought my butt off to be better and do better. I dug deep within and pulled out that lost, alone, terrified little girl who had died years ago. I allowed her to be reborn and I showed her where to find the peace she had been longing for all these years. It was up to me to give her a new life filled with trust, love, and forgiveness.

I had a passion and a drive to begin living, for the first time in my life. I wanted to be free from all anger and resentment. I wanted to soar high and live this amazing life guilt-free and with a heart full of love.

# CHAPTER SIX

# ONE STEP CAN CHANGE EVERYTHING

You will never change your life until you change something you do on a daily basis. If you find your life isn't perfect, then each morning when you wake up, you have two choices: You can stay in your current, disappointing situation or you can get up and chase the dreams you create about how you want your life to be!

If you are serious about changing unwanted habitual behaviors, you must replace them with the behaviors you do want—and you have to practice these new habits every day.

For example, you might want to address bad eating habits, overeating, not exercising every day, thinking negative thoughts, and so on. What we repeat over and over become habits, and this applies to both good behaviors and bad. If you repeat negative self-talk, you begin to act on those thoughts and carry them out through bad behaviors. On the other hand, if you implement healthy foods and movement into your life every day, these become habits. Before you know it, those unwanted habits or behaviors are a memory.

I started to make small changes on a daily basis. I physically wrote out a goal on paper and placed it where I could see it every day. When I decided to quit smoking, I knew I needed to replace this bad habit with a good habit. I chose running because I felt discouraged that I could not run. I had tried many times, and at first, I only made it a little way down the street or maybe around the block before I would quit. I hated how quickly I became winded. Well, that's what smoking two packs of cigarettes a day will do to the human body! But I did not give up. This time, I promised myself, I would not give up. I was determined to run one mile without stopping.

So each day, I would get up and run. And each day it got easier and easier. Soon, I was not craving the nicotine as much as I had before, and I was better able to endure the physical demands running placed on my body. Over a period of time, I actually began to enjoy the sport. I found that as I ran, I was able to clear my mind. I found this form of activity to be therapeutic. One day, I realized I was actually enjoying an activity that, only a few months earlier, I had dreaded. Between stopping smoking and getting some good exercise, I was beginning to feel less tired. I realized I could taste food again—and I also earned a tiny bit of self-confidence.

My goals started changing, the stronger I became. I decided I was ready to take on a half marathon. After the completion of my first race, I started training with more dedication. I became unstoppable. I decided I wanted to run a full marathon within the year. I trained hard but safely and accomplished my marathon within a few months of completing the half. Talk about a personal victory! I was participating in events I had once only dreamed of. My dreams were becoming a reality, based on the drive I had to become successful in everything I did.

I was fearless in my quest to find genuine happiness. Once I began to work on my emotional flaws, and started to understand where the internal pain was coming from, I created new habits. I slowly confronted my darkest past memories, feeling a sense of compassion and understanding for every situation. I replaced my worst habits with new, healthy habits, and over time, my life started changing direction.

When I stopped holding onto the past and all the pain that came with it, I moved into a life of peace and freedom—a life where there was light, color, and happiness. I was beginning to discover balance and how to maintain a healthy, happy, and stable life for myself by implementing positive thoughts and actions every day. I decided I was getting sick and tired of my own nonsense. It was time I faced reality and worked to find the answers I had longed for all of my life.

I knew that, if I did not do this for me, I would pretty much continue living the same way I had in previous years. From this moment, I began to fight like hell. I would not stop until I was winning at this life. I am pleased to be able to share with you how I did it, in the hopes you will be inspired to find the ways that work for you.

"The freeing ourselves of the unseen prison is a work to be taken seriously. I am undertaking this lesson with love and compassion tempered with honesty, humility, truth, strength, gratitude, and a knowing of when to be UN-serious. The more we are aware of our childhood wounds, possible trauma, sexual issues, blind spots, and actively work towards healing ourselves, the more we become objective with ourselves, without behaving mechanically and reactionary, the better we truly know ourselves. Know Thyself! However, knowing thyself also implies knowing our weaknesses, buffers and lies we're telling ourselves and may have for a very long time. This work cannot always be done alone for we need mirrors from others who see us at times better than we can see ourselves. Obviously it would help to have friends who are also engaged in sincere self-work, have basic understanding of psychology and are aware of 'the topic of all topics;' otherwise our friends may just support our buffers in their well-meaning intent to make ourselves feel better."

—Bernhard Guenther

# Step 1

*"We admitted we were powerless over our addictions—*
*that our lives became unmanageable."*

"The original quest for distraction from life's tensions and responsibilities, for relief from past guilt and present frustration, now led us to oblivion."

Think about this for a moment. Let it sink in. It took me multiple times of reading to truly understand it. From viewing life as "anything goes, who cares, nothing fazes me," this was a powerful statement and so true. I had been oblivious to how my actions would affect my life long-term. I was on a mission of distraction from any emotional attachment or responsibility for my actions. I could not feel or understand the ramifications that would come with making poor choices and bad decisions, time and time again.

Believe it or not, the first step was hard! Recognizing my original distraction from life and admitting I was powerless took practice and hard work. I continued writing, over and over, all the things that were out of my control until it sank in, until it was black and white. I had spent so much time worrying and depressed over things that had happened that were out of my control—things that no longer served a purpose—that my life was at a standstill. I was stuck, unable to move forward because I was constantly looking back with regrets.

Things I did not have the power to change:

1. My past

2. My parents

3. My mother's illness

4. Any abuse that I endured up until this point

5. What I had witnessed as a child, and all of the frightening scenes I had seen

6. All my previous mistakes

Admitting that I was not able to control past behaviors was a difficult task. Control was a habit for me, because that was the only sense of power I had held all of my life. I began to journal my thoughts and how I was feeling in the exact moments of writing. I continued to write every day. This would end up having a tremendous impact on my emotional healing.

Writing, internalizing, seeing, and reading my daily blogs out loud helped me to process all of the emotions. I now recommend this to all of my clients, especially when it includes changing habits, learning self-love, or simply finding themselves. Journaling helps us to "see" what we are feeling. Processing and admitting that our lives had become unmanageable takes practice, and it takes time for this awareness to sink in. Once it does, the places you revisit are not always pleasant—but they are a crucial part of completing all of the steps.

## Step 2

*"Came to believe that a power greater
than ourselves could restore our sanity."*

What we go through in the early stages of change is difficult. Once I discovered my spiritual connection to my higher power, I began to feel content. Now, when I mention the phrase "higher power," many turn their attention elsewhere. When I speak of a higher power, it means an object, person, place, GOD, or thing that you find peace and contentment with. Different people in our society have a variety of beliefs, and that is fine. As long as the individual's higher power is their way to a spiritual connection and peace—and to living a life of honest, genuine, and loving displays—it will work. It is our right to choose what form of power we connect with.

The idea is to find your spiritual connection to your GOD. Mine happens to be Christianity. I am not ashamed of loving my God. I find peace in giving God all of myself: good days, bad days, good choices, bad choices. It doesn't matter, I give it all to him. I follow the rules of his standards and not mine. I ask myself if my choices would be approved by him. This does not mean I am perfect. I still slip from time to time, but I find comfort and guidance from God.

I do not walk around preaching and throwing the Bible at everyone I meet, and I do not intend to preach about all the blessings that have come my way. God is good and he has given me a guardian angel more than enough times through my life. All the times in my teenage years and early adult life that I prayed for peace through death, God was there with all of his angels, protecting me.

As I began wanting to live more than anything, I was struck with a few life-threating diseases and illness over a span of ten years. As many years as I had spent praying for death, I spent fighting for life. See how funny life can be? The times I prayed for silence, it would not come, and the days I wanted nothing more than to live, the fear of dying was deafening. I can remember lying in the hospital bed praying to wake up the next morning and asking God to please give me another chance at life. I just assumed illness was "payback" for all the times I tried to intentionally end my own life. But it wasn't a payback—it was a lesson. To me, it was God's way of showing me how much I really did love this life.

Forget all your previous pain and heartaches, and find gratitude in your current life.

## Step 3

*"Made a decision to turn our will and our lives*
*over to the care of God as we understood God."*

I began opening my eyes to the way I was and how I had been treated as a child. I began to turn all of my hate and resentment over to God. All of my unanswered questions about why certain things had happened to me were answered when I connected myself to him. The answers were, none of those things had been my fault. The things I'd witnessed were not my fault. The anger I was expressing was out of fear. Fear had consumed me from the age of four until I was thirty-nine years old—fear of failing, fear of living, fear of rejection, fear of life. You name it, I feared it. I was the most insecure young lady on the planet, or so I thought.

I was able to heal and find forgiveness not only for those who hurt me, but for myself, as well. I wasn't justifying their behaviors—I was understanding them. I developed empathy for all who had hurt me. They, too, had obviously been hurting. I found love for my parents and understood they had done the best they could. I have forgiven all who hurt me, because without the events that took place in my life, I would not be the woman I am today. I let go of all the hurt and anger, putting it in a place that no longer deserved attention, a place I no longer needed to visit. It saved my life.

My love and passion for life soared. I was flying high on life. I made amends with most people, and for those whom I haven't spoken with physically, it has been done in my heart. I understand my actions were built on a foundation of mistrust and childhood trauma and insecurities at a very young age. Now I was teaching myself to feel love, contentment, loyalty, honesty, and consequence.

## Step 4

*"Made a searching and fearless moral inventory of ourselves."*

It's hard to understand people we do not know. When we have a lack of true understanding about ourselves, we find it hard to convey empathy toward another human being. Unless we are willing to make the sacrifice of discovering ourselves and understanding what we represent, we will continue to be at war, not only with ourselves but with everyone around us. Moving forward is impossible when we find ourselves disconnected to the world and all those who live in it.

Growing up, I was taught to put up with injustice and just shut up. I kept my head down and my eyes closed so no one could see the pain that was living inside me.

When I first read Step 4, I could not understand the meaning of "moral inventory." I had been searching for answers and trying to achieve a real understanding about myself for a very long time, only to discover that I could not explain anything about myself or my actions so far. Apparently, taking an inventory of my values, morals, and the motives behind every situation I was not proud of would help me to understand.

As I began explaining myself to myself, I sometimes had to create a softer scenario, because the truth was hard to swallow. I was leaving out parts of the truth because I could not digest some of the things I had done in previous years. The truth was too hard to admit. As I began writing an inventory of each situation I felt guilty or ashamed about, I recognized my part in manipulating and my lack of self-control. I had always felt the need to control everyone and everything. If something did not go my way, I made sure it did, in the end. I did not accept losing anyone or anything.

I was finding so many things I already knew but had never allowed myself to fully see. I began asking myself, what was I hiding? Why wouldn't I allow myself to accept my mistakes?

Shame.

Guilt.

Fear.

As I continued my honest and true inventory of unpleasant memories, I slowly owned all my faults. Each one was brought to the surface, where I was forced to examine my actions. After writing down each one of my flaws, hurtful actions, and bad behaviors, I read them aloud. I then had to process my intentions and turn them into a learning experience, to teach myself why my behaviors had hurt others.

I also needed to understand the motives behind my actions. I took all of my notes to my next therapy session. I wanted to understand this more than anything at the time. As I uncovered personal and intimate details about myself, I found that I did not like these things one bit. I put things into perspective by asking, how would I feel if someone did those things to me or to one of my children? I decided at that exact moment that I would change all of those bad behaviors. I made a promise to myself to always ask God for guidance if I felt weak or vulnerable to any temptations to act out.

One by one, each of my faults were replaced with good, healthy actions. These actions would benefit and help all of those around me. I was driven to do wonderful things for others, and I never skipped a beat during the self-changing process. I learned how to divert my coping mechanisms from previous pain to self-love and forgiveness by taking action and doing great things to help others in a positive way. Each unwanted behavior was replaced with a positive and beneficial behavior.

I discovered I did not have to stay stuck and unable to move or change from my existing circumstances. I was more than a product of all of those bad experiences. I understood that the bad things that had happened would never go away, but I was not going to be chained to those memories for one more day.

## Step 5

*"Admitted to God, to ourselves, and to another
human being the exact nature of our wrongs."*

Like it or not, I was faced with the hard truth. I was responsible for ALL of my relationships, positive and negative, that I had created or attracted. It was time for me to take responsibility for all of it and understand that only I had the power to change them. I had been a victim of unjust circumstances, yes, but I did not want to continue my life playing the role of a victim.

We can blame others until we're blue in the face, but this was keeping me from moving past my previous circumstances. It was stifling my personal growth. You just can't have a healthy relationship with anyone unless you have a healthy relationship with yourself first.

Up until this point, I was recognizing my behaviors and owning up to my wrongdoings. But now I had to tell God—and another person! It was up to me to be open, honest, and truthful. This step would be a major setback for me. I went back and forth and back, over and over again, attempting to write down my version of things, but I left out critical components, out of pure embarrassment.

As I read Step 5 again, it slowly began to sink in. This was a necessary requirement. I found that I not only needed to do this, I wanted to do this. With each new journal entry, I disclosed more and more truth about each circumstance. My writing was open, honest, and without effort. This was a humbling experience. I knew I needed to take action and begin to face each of my wrongdoings with the confidence that the guilt, shame, and embarrassment would soon be self-forgiven.

Oh, the fear and anxiety was unbearable leading up to my releasing all of this to another! I knew I needed to tell my therapist first. I wondered how she would react to my truth and how well I would explain it.

The day arrived, and I resolved to do my very best. I took a breath and started with my story, telling it as completely and as genuinely as I knew how. As I heard myself speaking nothing but truth, an unfamiliar sensation swept over me. I could feel it in every ounce of my being. It felt like a ton of bricks had been lifted off my shoulders. Wow, just like that, it was spilling over into the room like a movie. I was experiencing an immense sense of relief. It was AMAZING what telling the truth could do. I certainly was not proud of my actions, but I owned up to every one of them.

After that session had ended, it was time to have a conversation with one of the most important people in my life: my husband.

We sat down to talk, and I revealed all of the past abuse and my childhood experiences. Most importantly, I told my husband of my wrongdoings during the weeks leading up to my stay at MBR. I wanted him to blame me, not anyone else. For six months, I had been screwing up, doing anything I could to push him away.

It was his turn to react. Up until this point, I'd never spoken of the details of trauma or abuse I had endured growing up. He knew I'd had a rough beginning at life, but not details. It is embarrassing for me to speak of the events, and it was almost unbearable to relive them, but I knew I could not go one more day keeping all of this from him.

He knew about the disturbance I had created within our marriage. Now I needed to take full responsibility for my actions. He was never to blame. He had been perfect. As I began to explain my need to be rejected and my desire for personal destruction, his reaction took me by surprise. I expected him to push me away, and maybe even file for a divorce. I anticipated yelling and screaming, but he did none of these things.

He held me tightly as we cried together. He promised to never leave or hurt me. He swore he was not like anyone who had harmed me in the past. He was my husband and he would be with me until the end. For once in my life, someone other than me knew *everything* about me.

It felt crazy to think I deserved any of this. I understand now that I do. I deserve this man and everything he brings to our marriage and family! I welcome our healthy relationship, and the happiness that follows is real and natural.

We had many therapy sessions following this, but with each new session, our relationship grew stronger and better than ever. When I find myself asking how I deserve this, I remind myself that I am worth all of it!

# Step 6

*"Were entirely ready to have God remove
all of these defects of character."*

The idea of surrendering my faults and defects was going to be easy, right? No, this was a challenging step. This step would take me months to get through.

*"Whenever you find yourself doubting how far you can
go, just remember how far you have come. Remember
everything you have faced, all the battles you have
won, and all of the fears you have overcome."*

—Unknown

Changing my previous behaviors into positive behaviors took dedication and work. This would be a daily goal of mine, and one over which I took ownership. I gave up many things, but there was one thing that would prevent me from moving forward. I was stuck each time I tried to let go of controlling everyone and everything around me.

I tried to justify the control by implying it was good for others to do things my way. I felt my way was so much better than their way. I found myself discouraged and stagnant, really reluctant to give this fault of mine to anyone else. I was not willing to feel the ramifications of letting go of control and becoming vulnerable on all levels of humanity. This seemed an impossible task. It wasn't that I couldn't do this, but I really did not want to. I'd spent most of my childhood with very little control over situations and the circumstances of my abuse. During the worst times of my life, someone else had been in control.

The older I got, the more I discovered that I could take control. It gave me a feeling of power I'd never had growing up. Because most of my childhood situations were out of my control, and I'd had absolutely no control over all the bad things that happened, I found comfort in controlling everything. If I gave up control now, what would happen?

Step 6 was asking me to give this over to my higher power. I made several attempts to hand this defect over, but each time, it was a fail. I sat stuck here for many months, trying to give up this one thing. I became so discouraged at one point that I almost quit all the steps in their entirety.

Then one day, my oldest daughter and I had the worst fight ever. I was not able to rationalize the situation, because I knew I was losing this argument. Now remember, until now, whenever I felt I had lost control, a downward path of personal destruction would follow. This was the worst fight I had ever experienced with any of my children—or with anyone, for that matter.

I know teenagers will test and try a parent's boundaries, but something about this argument was different. It led to months of separation from her. Nothing I said could persuade her to listen to the demands I placed on her. I was trying to make her choose what I thought was best for her, and she was not budging. This sent me over the edge with anger and disappointment. I could not understand why she was unable to see that I had her best interests at heart and her well-being in mind all along. I was losing control over my daughter, who would soon turn eighteen.

Things only got worse. The more I tried to control the situation, the more she slipped away.

After she graduated high school, I remember giving her a choice: she had to either obey the rules I had implemented for her own well-being or she could stay living with her father. I had placed my family smack in the middle of this situation in the first place, and now I was telling my daughter she could not have anything to do with certain people. She chose to continue the relationships she had with her friends, no matter how much I tried to persuade her to stay away from them.

I now realize that she was taking control of her own life. Because I had been controlling everything she did, she wanted to prove she was able to make decisions for herself. I could not comprehend this at the time because I was unwilling to let go of my need to control. I became consumed with anger and found it hard to speak to her. Despite all the years I had spent protecting my children from harm, I was not able to protect her this time. She chose to do what she felt was best for her.

Throughout this episode of my life, I felt overwhelming grief and loss. How could I lose my daughter over this? I began to process the situation and write down why I was so angry and upset, but I had trouble gaining clarity because the communication between us was so strained. My relationship with my daughter was shaky. I remember walking into her bedroom, which she had not been in for weeks, and putting things away; when I opened her drawer, I began to cry so hard that my son heard me. I could not stop crying. The pain I felt over losing my daughter at this time was unbearable. I could not snap out of it. I longed for her to be small again, when things between us were so much different. I missed the times when I was her world and she loved me. My heart was broken. I missed my daughter so much that I felt I could not breathe.

After sitting in her bedroom for hours, going through all of her things, smelling her perfumes and looking at pictures, something swept over me without warning. I felt guilty about the argument, guilt for my actions, and guilt for how I reacted to her need to have a sense of freedom and control over her own life. I was such an idiot! Had I just given up this fault months ago, my daughter would still be here! I came to understand why Step 6 was so crucial to my healing. I had to give up my need to control everyone and everything in order to salvage any future relationship I would have with my child.

At that exact moment, the decision was made. I was done! It was time to hand this one over to my higher power and start practicing ways to implement resolution to the outcomes of my actions. From that moment, I began working my butt off and taking all necessary steps to give up my need to control.

I practiced with my other children. It started with their bedrooms. I had always cleaned and organized their things, but I realized during this step that this issue involved their personal space and freedom. I needed to allow them to have their own space and take care of it whatever way they felt was necessary. Their rooms were a mess; they had food and drinks and clothes everywhere, and no organization at all. But it was their space, and they loved it. From then on, if I found myself getting anxious over a mess when I walked by, I closed their bedroom doors.

It was a start, but this road was long. The habit of control was deeply ingrained. My daughter and I have reconciled now, but that argument was a learning experience for me. Even though I continue to set boundaries for my other two children, I allow them much more freedom of choice. I still find myself struggling over wanting to control, but it is so much better now. I work every day to make sure I never forget what can happen if you are not willing to change.

I made a promise to myself to NEVER allow my need to control to come between me and the ones I love the most: my children and my husband. I was so inspired by the Serenity Prayer throughout my treatment that it is now tattooed on my shoulder. I begin each day with this prayer and I end each night with it.

"Dear God, grant me the serenity to accept the things I cannot change, courage to change the things I can, and the wisdom to know the difference."

# Step 7

*"Humbly asked God to remove our shortcomings."*

"Allowing oneself to feed into the chaos around you is only the distortion of your mind in wanting you to feel the need to debate and argue about things that only set up to keep you in the illusion of fear. This conditioning of the mind is only a deception that has been taught to you from those that want to keep you in control in not allowing you the free will to become who you truly are.

To leave these distortions and become the loving light you are gives you the peace to become the fully conscious being of source. Where the outer distortions do not control who you are. You are the source of unconditional love, not the chaos of the mind.

Be free of those thoughts that keep you from rising into your loving presence and feel the peace within."

—Mary Long

In order to continue moving forward with my life in a positive manner, I realized I had to remove all shortcomings every day. By continuously exercising my spiritual connections, I slowly began to search for all the positivity in my life. I began giving thanks for every situation, person, place, and thing that had been a part of my journey. This may sound crazy, but as I began to give thanks for every dimension of my being, I found myself thanking God for every situation in my life thus far. Without all of the bad, I don't think I would have been so passionate about this life and helping others. My passion, and my drive to give hope to those who feel there is none, is driven by how far I have come.

I never dreamed I would be living the life I am today. Positivity and happiness is contagious. I am now open to personal connections and allow myself to have healthy relationships with others. I surround myself with uplifting and positive people who will influence me in a good, healthy way.

There was a time when I would not allow hugging or any form of physical affection by anyone. I now welcome all of it. I am comfortable showing emotion, giving affection and also receiving it. This takes practice. You must constantly remind yourself to let your guard down and remember that it's okay to be vulnerable in safe situations. The past will not and cannot hurt you if you don't allow it to.

I have opened my heart, and if I am rejected, oh well. Such is life, right? I do not hold fear on the highest level of priorities. It is now at the bottom. I love my new-found freedom and the personal connections I have built and am continuing to build. This life is truly amazing!

## Step 8

*"Made a list of all persons we had harmed,
and became willing to make amends to them all."*

"Forgiveness does not mean that we suppress our anger; forgiveness means that we have asked for a miracle: the ability to see through the mistakes that someone has made to the truth that lies in all of our hearts. There is no peace without forgiveness. If you can state, despite your resistance, your willingness to see the spiritual innocence, the light in the soul of the one who has harmed you, you have begun the journey to a deep and unshakable peace."

—Marianne Williamson

I'm going to be completely honest: this list was not a small list. It was a list that took up many lines in my journal. Throughout my life, I had hurt people without understanding what the outcome of my actions would be. I did not intentionally cause anyone pain, but my actions certainly did. I did not understand the consequences of what I was doing when I did things that were hurtful to people. As I began to write down all the people I'd hurt, I felt guilt, shame, and embarrassment. And with that, I began to cry.

Because I was now in a place where I felt so different than when I had done those things, I began to slip back into the self-hate mode. I asked questions: "How could I? What in the world was I thinking? Who am I?" I began to feel sad and as if I was not worth all the good I was now seeing in my life. I didn't deserve to be happy after all the pain I had caused.

I can remember having a hard time getting myself motivated to walk into my studio and train my clients. I was in negative mode and felt unworthy of all of it. And then it happened.

I was shopping at a local store when I saw someone I had harmed in the past. I don't mean physically harmed, but I had lied to them. I decided to walk up and challenge this step once and for all. As I approached them, I began to shake and had trouble moving. The closer I got, the more I could hear myself breathing. And then, there I was, standing in front of her. I reached out and hugged her, unsure of the outcome. But it was something that seemed natural in that moment.

Her reaction at first was hesitant, which was to be expected. As we stood facing one another, she smiled and reassured me that it was okay to proceed with the conversation. We spoke for a few brief moments. As I pulled away in my car, I was crying uncontrollably. I remembered feeling the pain of what I had done. I felt a sense of relief now, but I also felt something I had not felt before: empathy.

For the next few days, I did some serious soul-searching. I really had to struggle to get out of my funk. It took every ounce of mental strength I had to pull out of it. But now I knew I was capable of being thoughtful and kind and having remorse for my bad actions.

"At any given moment, you have the power to say: This is not how the story is going to end."

## Step 9
*"Made direct amends to such people (from Step 8) wherever possible, except when to do so would injure them or others."*

Step 9 sounds very similar to the previous one, but it is not. Here is where you come face-to-face with the people you have hurt.

"Speak in such a way that others love to listen to you. Listen in such a way that others love to speak to you."

Throughout this process, I learned that I misunderstood others most of the time. I really didn't have an understanding, up until this point, of how to communicate my thoughts and feelings. Because anger was at the foundation of who I was, I always expressed my thoughts in a hateful manner. I was unable to control conversations without "blowing up" or talking down to others, even when they did not deserve to be screamed at. This was a learned behavior and one of my worst habits. Having a calm conversation was difficult because I clearly could not process my emotions in the moment.

I began practicing speech and conversations with others. When I was angry or hurt, I knew I had to speak calmly and convey my message in a kind way in order to keep my listener focused on our conversation. I still find myself speaking out of anger, but now I am able to choose what I say by controlling my emotions as I am speaking. Before this, I had never wanted to hear what the other person in the conversation was saying. I would tune them out and quite honestly dismiss their words as if they didn't matter. When I opened my ears to what others were saying, I began to learn how to listen, understand, and open the lines of communication.

When you read Step 8, you immediately think, "apologize"—right? Well, not only is an apology necessary, but you must open yourself to the possibility of being rejected by the people you are attempting to make amends with. Please understand that not everyone will accept this. They may be holding on to the hurt you caused to them and might not be capable of forgiving you. You must be willing to accept this reality.

Completing this step will not end all of the pain you may have caused to another. To be honest, that pain may never go away for them. However, this was certainly a way for me to truly understand what consequences my actions had produced. It put me on the path of learning to accept my mistakes.

During this step, I made a "forever promise" to God and to myself that I would never hurt another human being, as long as I live. I would stop the disruptive actions that had caused others so much pain.

## Step 10

*"Continued to take a personal inventory and when we were wrong, promptly admitted it."*

Change will never happen overnight. Practice, consistency, repetition, and commitment will always lead to positive results.

"The ones who are crazy enough to think they can change the world, are usually the ones that do."

I have been up and down the mountains of consciousness again and again throughout my life and during the last few weeks. I've walked down the darkest streets of anger, rage, and explosive behaviors, which always led to distraction and disaster. As I clean out my baggage and heartache, I am focusing on love, understanding, forgiveness, pure honesty, and compassion. I am finding freedom from recurring nightmares as I continue to build a life based on truth and awareness.

I can better relate to every woman's pain and every man's sorrows. I can see that, by allowing these emotions, I can fully understand them, process them, and own them. I realize what my feelings truly are and use them in ways to benefit all those around me.

After going far enough down the dark hole of suffering, I now rise up from judgment and ridicule. I have been putting things into perspective as to just how small people can allow themselves be. When others judge and badmouth me without truly having an understanding of who I am, I forgive them, because they know no better. I used to become so hurt from someone else's choices and actions toward me. Now I no longer allow them to impact how my day will go.

After fighting for what seemed an eternity, I still sometimes find myself right in the midst of pain and suffering, consumed with feelings that I am less than I really am. I try to remember that I am no less than when I was born. I am complete, whole, divine, strong, aware, human, and imperfect—and I am enough!

I will continue to shine my light on others who have forgotten how wonderful they are.

I constantly remind myself of how I want to live and how I need to live. I simply move past the hard days with the strength and courage of knowing I am good and I deserve to be happy.

Part of my personal inventory was an examination of my goals. Whatever personal goals you have designed for yourself, always make sure they are attainable, or else they will set you up to fail. I had to learn the hard way on this one. You will not lose twenty pounds in a week. In fact, losing weight too quickly is not going to be effective long-term; most likely, the weight will come back, plus bring with it an additional ten pounds. Going to church every Sunday will not make you a saint. Following the rules of your higher power will give you guidelines, consequences, and a belief in new beginnings. Attainable, genuine, and honest goals have wonderful outcomes.

If you are passionate about your intentions, they will not only benefit your life but also the lives of those around you. A personal, attainable goal may be to lose twenty pounds over three months. Setting it up in realistic timing will give you more energy to keep up with your children and be more active throughout the day. You may want to quit smoking in order to make it up a flight of steps without feeling like you are half dead and your chest is going to burst. Laziness has no room during your personal inventory. Be sure to check, adjust, and improve all actions every day to earn personal success.

If you have not reached your goal, evaluate your actions. Take all goals seriously and don't wonder why the results are not present when you have not done the work. Take responsibility for the outcome.

## Step 11

*"Sought through prayer and meditation to improve our conscious contact with a power greater than ourselves, praying only for knowledge of God's will for us and the power to carry that out."*

I have realized that there is a greater power than just me. My spiritual connection to God has given me a conscious relationship with someone much greater.

> "Find wholeness and balance within the depths
> of your own being and then watch the divine
> reflection manifest in the outer world."
> —Openhand

Prayer and meditation create a place for me to just be me. I may be happy, sad, having a bad day or a good day, but there is always room in my day for prayer and meditation. The first time I tried to meditate, I found it impossible to shut my mind off and allow nothing but silence into my thoughts. It took many attempts, and it still takes practice to just be still, present, and in that exact moment.

When I first began to mediate, I would sit in a quiet place trying to eliminate all distractions. The more I practiced, the better I began to feel. At one time, silence used to frighten me. It would take me back to horrible times of my childhood and slip me quickly into a very dark scene. Meditation has taught me to feel comfortable being still. Allowing myself to fully relax is rejuvenating; it gives my mind and body the necessary breaks they long for. The mental focus and practice has allowed me to control my thoughts, and they are much clearer now. Here are a few simple steps you can do to begin the practice of meditation.

1. Find a quiet place where there are no external distractions.
2. Sit in an upright position that is comfortable for you.
3. Set a timer for no more than ten minutes.
4. Get comfortable.
5. Bring your attention to your breath only. Close your mouth and focus on your breath coming in through the nose and out through the nose. If your mind begins to wander, which it will, take your focus back to your breath. If you find it difficult to concentrate, try counting. Relax and don't stress if you feel you are not able to shut off your mind. The more you practice, the easier it becomes.

## Step 12

*"Having had a spiritual awakening as a result of these steps, we tried to carry this message to others and to practice these principles in all areas of our lives."*

"All pain, trauma, addiction and disease are raw material from which our consciousness awakening is formed. The experience of walking through the pain (utilizing the tools available, whether they be therapy, treatment, bodywork, journaling, etc.) is a journey of healing which moves us from darkness into light. This journey is multi–dimensional, transcending the limiting experiences of pain and embracing the divine self within each of us. The journey through the "valley of the shadow" can bring us from the depths of desperate limitation to the heights of expressing the fullness of our humanity. This is our birthright."

—The Healing Dimensions

I did not, by any means, begin to preach to my loved ones, friends, clients, or anyone else. However, I convey my beliefs by expression of actions. This means I began to practice what I believed. I try to be a positive role model to everyone I come into contact with each day. I express my gratitude every day and look at my life as a blessing, no matter what type of day I had. I post, blog, and express positivity and contagious happiness through all of my writings. My spiritual connection and consciousness has lead me to a very peaceful place. I connect each day and check in throughout the day to ensure I am keeping myself on track and within my personal expectations.

"Give God your weakness and he'll give you his strength."

# CHAPTER SEVEN

# TAKE YOUR DREAMS SERIOUSLY

"A dream is just a dream, but a goal is a
dream with a plan and a due date."
—Harvey Mackay

With awareness, we have the potential to control our lives. If we don't like the path we are on or the life we are living, we must get off and change it! Yes, change it!

No matter what the arena—sports, health, fitness, career, relationships—there is always a point when we must make a CHOICE about how far we want to go down the road to success.

When you find yourself in that moment of choice, remember, you can take the easy road and keep getting the same results you've always gotten—or you can take the more challenging road and find out just how amazing it feels to reach goals and succeed. The mind gives up before the body does, but only if you LET IT.

Let's look at a great athlete; what we see is a result. What we don't see is the dedication, the hours, the sacrifice, and the commitment that went into creating that greatness. Those people who judge the success of another in a negative way often fail to see the hard work and commitment it took to become successful.

## ACHIEVING YOUR GOALS

**1. Define what you want.**

This is often the hardest part. Your mind will try to protect you from the unknown by telling you things like, "It's not a good time right now," or "I can wait one more day." None of your excuses matter at all when measured against the days you have to spend living your life.

**2. Look at the big picture and write it down.**

We are all artists and the world is our own canvas. You have to write your goals down. Look at them and read them until they're real. Write them in a journal or anywhere you can see them. Read them and embed them into your mind. We all have a purpose in life—we just need to fulfill it.

**3. Strategize.**

Break up the big picture into actionable steps that you can focus on in the immediate future. Becoming a martial arts master requires isolated training of different body parts, terrains, styles of combat, and mental strategy. You don't do all of those things in one day. Identify the elements that are necessary to accomplish your goals and set a schedule for each of them.

One of the biggest excuses I used to have for not taking the necessary steps toward reaching my goals was "I have too many bills to pay to take the time to work on this." When I decided to get serious about achieving goals, I set up an accelerated bill payoff strategy that included living without a car for six months.

Where there's a will, there's a way. Yes, you will sometimes make some sacrifices. And yes, when you get focused, your priorities might not make sense to anyone but you. That's just fine. All you have to do is remember the parts of your life that you need to change and remember the big picture.

**4. Give your goals a time frame.**

Perturbation—or "mental agitation"—is one of the most important elements in goal-setting. We need to be agitated enough about our present condition to pursue a change. I have learned this the hard way throughout my life. Once you change your mindset, you change your life.

When setting your goals, give yourself a specific time frame in which you're going to complete them. It needs to be soon enough that you begin to feel the changes you're making becoming real, and just long enough to give you time to take care of all of the details. The deadline pressure will push you to get after it on a Saturday or a Tuesday night instead of watching TV or surfing the internet—which might be exactly the difference that it takes to get you there.

**5. Choose your friends and social networks carefully.**

The people with whom we spend our time influence the direction we take. We rub off on other people, too. One of the best things I have learned is, I have just as much power to influence how someone feels as they have on me. Positive encouragement goes a long way. Setting a good example will be a positive influence on our children, family, and friends. My siblings are both thriving and doing extremely well today. They both have careers, are married, and have beautiful, healthy children of their own. My three children are doing amazing as well. My oldest daughter is a junior in college and currently attends Miseracordia University. She will graduate in 2018 with her bachelor's degree in nursing. My middle child is a junior in high school and is uncertain of what she will choose as her major in college. But I know when she decides, she will surprise us all. She is a funny, outgoing, and a free-spirited child. She loves life and isn't afraid to tell you what she is feeling. My son is in fifth grade and wishes to one day be a professional athlete. His drive and determination are contagious. As a mother, I enjoy watching my children grow into such amazing human beings. They are confident, loving, and just great kids. I know they will grow up and do wonderful things in life, and for this I am truly blessed.

## 6. Don't succumb to negative self-talk.

I hear people say things every day that ultimately hold them back from true success. "I'm bad at this." "I suck at relationships." "No one would ever listen to me." We create our own reality. Get out of that mindset and stop putting yourself down. Remember that our minds play tricks on us. We can become what we think. BE CAREFUL with this one!

## 7. Fall down. Get up. Repeat.

Don't let the bumps in the road and setbacks derail you from your purpose. Accept them and keep going.

I have a personal goal of completing the Super Spartan race. It may not seem like a big deal to some, but it is my goal and it is huge to me. To prepare myself, I have added significant features to my everyday training to build my endurance and my core, arm, and leg strength. I can't tell you how many times I have fallen in life. But I always get up. I always finish and I never give up!

If we aren't able to look beyond our current situations, we will miss incredible opportunities. Dreams can certainly become realities. There are possibilities everywhere. You just need to find them and believe in them.

Using everything I had learned in MBR and implementing the Twelve Steps each and every day, I have learned how to live. I've learned how to feel. I have learned how to be honest and true, to show emotion, to feel empathy, and to love with all of my heart. I began to feel free from a past that used to haunt me. I have found my passion and my commitment to helping others.

As I began to get comfortable with my true nature, I started posting and blogging bits and pieces of my life on all of my social media pages. The bold truth no longer scares me. It is what it is, and I can't change it. What I can change is how I live each and every day from here on out.

As I continue surrounding myself with positive people and putting myself in situations that will only benefit me and my family, I continue growing and learning. Life is always about learning. You must be willing to accept your imperfections and move on.

I understand that the more I took responsibility for my own happiness and went after my goals and dreams with all my might, the more I attracted people who were on a similar path. I also attracted things that made my life even more enjoyable.

Once I was truly and deeply happy, the wonderful people and things I attracted were bonuses that enhanced my happiness. I stopped relying on temporary fixes and other people for my own personal happiness. I became the source of my joy.

It was time to make amends with my mother and to meet face-to-face. We had spoken very little over the years. I had kept my distance because our relationship was toxic and had damaging effects on me. I decided to jump on a plane to Florida and face her with open communication, compassion, love, and an understanding of who she was and why.

Being around my mother as the "new me" was liberating. I had already forgiven her, but I had a new sense of compassion for her behaviors and her illness. As I looked at her sitting directly across from me, feelings of remorse and guilt consumed me. I felt guilty for hating her and being so angry with her for so many years.

Having a profound understanding of her situation and what she had gone through had opened my heart to feel empathy and compassion toward her. There was a time when I'd been unable to hear her voice or even look at her. Throughout my entire life, family and friends had asked why I was so cold to my mother. But I had been unable to forgive my parents until I could understand myself.

Through therapy in Malibu and discovering my true self by working the Twelve Steps, I found I blamed my mom for what happened to me when she became sick. I also blamed my father for abandoning me and never seeing the signs that I was being abused. I was so angry with both of my parents because I needed someone to blame.

However, now I blame no one for the mistakes I made. I choose to take full responsibility for my manipulative behaviors, deceitful actions, unjustified arguments with others, and actions I took that disrupted the lives of people who were close to me.

I never went into detail about the past, the abuse, or my life with my parents. I was embarrassed and ashamed of all of it. Some relatives had tried to force me to be kind and affectionate toward my mother, but their attempts never worked. I had been deeply hurt, and my wounds needed to heal before I could move forward with any form of relationship. I knew I would face her when I was ready. Now, I felt it was time.

I have accepted that I will never have a close relationship with my mother in which we speak to one another every day or every week. I have come to terms with that. There are just some things that you must keep in the distance so that you can keep moving forward and preserve your sanity. You can't change people; you can only change yourself and how you react to them. My mother and I have spoken about my feelings and anger towards her many times throughout my adult life. It always ends in arguing, screaming, and tears with no resolution. She has apologized many times and I have tried to make amends as well. I do forgive her, but some people do not know how to stop unintentionally hurting you and I have accepted this. You cannot change people.

I am thankful for all of the challenges I faced growing up because each one of them was a disguised blessing. I am goal-oriented and driven by positive actions. I have a strong passion and commitment to help others.

I spent most of my life living in hell with no end in sight. But I am here to tell you there is always a way out. You have to climb and take each new day one step at a time. Hold on to all hope, and never give up on your life. So many opportunities are waiting for you, but you have to believe you are worth a better life!

One of the most important things I have learned is that being happy is a very personal thing and has nothing to do with anyone else. No one can make you happy. Happiness always will come from within. I never imagined my life could be as wonderful as it is now. I'd had dreams and I'd created images in my mind of what peace was like; now I am living those images with the beautiful house with a white fence, a husband who is everything I dreamed of, and children who are my best success to date.

Success will never be handed to you on a silver platter. If you want to be successful, you need to get off your butt, get out there, and make it happen. If I didn't agree with what they told me in school, I went out to learn more. I made sure I researched and then incorporated all of my education into my personal life.

I spent many years regretting my wrongdoings and covering my face in shame. For a long time, I didn't know what my purpose was. But that never stopped me from continuing to look for my purpose and follow my heart.

When you are on the right path, you just know it. Everything falls into place at the exact moment you least expect it to. I no longer run and hide from people.

The way to express our gratitude for life is by truly living. Don't hide from your past, because we all have one. Take ownership of all of your mistakes. Be humble with your success and stand proud of all that you have become.

I can remember getting up to teach my first fitness class, more than a decade ago. I was so shy and insecure, and for some reason, I would hold myself back. I realized this hesitancy for living had been affecting me for many years. I knew it was time to proceed without caution, hesitation, or regret—to just jump in with all of the passion that was driving me to help others. I had placed doubt and fear in my mind and shackled myself by limiting my capabilities for too long. It was time to leap forward and take control of my negative and insecure thoughts.

When I was a client myself, I would stand in the back of class, praying no one would see me. The first few weeks of teaching my classes were awful. I was a mess, struggling to implement my knowledge in this hour of fitness. I had so much trouble being in the front of the room. But as the weeks passed, my confidence grew, as well as my client base. My groups increased from just a handful of participants to a room full people wanting to take my class. They were having fun and they were seeing results.

The confidence I was gaining led me to reveal my true and honest personality in all of my sessions. I started having a blast! I grew comfortable with my skills and what I had learned, and it motivated me to keep learning and growing. I wanted to change how people viewed fitness and exercise. I was taking multiple online classes each year to further my education because I wanted to give my clients programs that worked and that they would look forward to.

I immersed myself in education and practiced for hours a day. I was driven to find the formulas that anyone could use to gain results. Could I finally have found my purpose in this life? It certainly felt that way. I was enjoying my new career as I slowly began building an empire of followers in the fitness industry. People were looking to me for help and guidance on their journeys.

I started to take my dreams seriously! I learned to not only dream big, but to validate my dreams as well.

My coaching was always about more than just weight loss. It was about helping others know they are not alone in an individual struggle and helping them find balance and create healthy changes. I believe that food and exercise choices are the key to mental clarity, hormone balance, increased energy levels, and maintaining a healthy weight.

I practice what I preach to all of my clients. I may have a slip here and there with my food, or I may skip a workout sometimes, but I always jump right back on the wagon. I don't let myself stray off my plan for too long, because I know how hard it can be to get back on track.

Being a health and fitness professional is something I take very seriously. I stand behind every recipe and workout session because they were designed out of love for the client and based on knowledge of the health and fitness industry. I always present the content with their best interests at heart. This is my way of giving to others so they can experience personal satisfaction and taste the wonderful flavor of a win.

We all deserve to be happy and healthy and to feel amazing! My programs are built around the truth that one size does not and will never "fit all." The number on the scale is not equivalent to your success. Success is how you feel and the new goals you are setting and accomplishing. It is about your overall state of well-being and happiness. Becoming comfortable in your own skin will take practice—but you can do this!

We all respond to change differently. How we react to change must be considered as part of any health- and fitness-related goals we aim to achieve.

As I began to study and implement the Four Seasons programs, I took many things into consideration such as expense, environment, availability of seasonal foods based on global crops, and economics. I was specific in choosing foods, spices, and ingredients that will trigger healthy hormone growth, enhance energy levels, and rid the body of any unwanted toxins that have built up over years of eating processed garbage, taking medicines, and drug use. It took me many years to create the perfect formulas.

If you are looking to change your eating habits, implement exercise, and feel happy, my Four Seasons Fitness Programs might be the answer for you. You must want to do this for you and no one else. You must want this more than anything else in order to achieve success.

Feeling great looks amazing on all of us!

Get out there and own your life like a boss!

Don't wait for "special occasions"—get up and live this beautiful life. Being alive is a blessing and a pretty good occasion, if you ask me.

Remember to keep moving forward with one attainable goal at a time. Before you know it, your way of thinking will have changed and you will discover true happiness.

Good luck to all of you! I will be here with you every step of the way.

# ABOUT ME

During my childhood and teenage years, I gained a lot of weight, lost a lot of weight, and I had absolutely no self-esteem. In my twenties, I lost my first marriage, my home, and my self-respect. I hit bottom for the first time in my adult life.

Then, fifteen years later, I followed the same path and hit bottom yet again. I slipped into a deep depression driven by anxiety from childhood trauma and, I was to learn later, PTSD.

I had always found comfort in unhealthy fatty and sugary foods. Self-loathing followed with every pound I gained. In high school, I was made fun of for being "the chubby girl," "fat," "Popeye," and other names too painful to repeat. After high school, I went on the "no food" diet: anorexia, diet pills, and laxatives. I could not get skinny enough.

I had my first wake-up call when I was eighteen years old while my sister and I were vacationing in Caracas, Venezuela. I was so addicted to laxatives and diet stimulants that I began to bleed internally and experience excruciating abdominal pain. Back in the U.S., I was admitted to a hospital where an MRI showed I had a small tear in my lower intestinal track and rectum. That incident scared me so much that I never touched another laxative—but I continued to take energy enhancers and appetite suppressants.

Going back and forth from skinny to heavy, abusing diet pills and binge eating, was mentally exhausting, but I couldn't stop it. My condition was hidden and went untreated for years. I married in my early twenties and had my first child. Life calmed down, emotionally, for a short time and I started nursing school.

While in college full time, being a wife and mother, everything began to spiral out of control again. It wasn't until years later that I discovered the meaning of addiction. Addiction is not only about illegal drugs and alcohol—it is about anything you do in excess and can't control. In January of 2014, I discovered I was an addict who suffered from PTSD related to early childhood abuse.

Wow, that was a hard thing to swallow! I continued to believe it was not true. How could I be an addict? I had never used street drugs and I don't drink often. But I discovered I had an addiction to anything that would make my internal pain go away and numb my feelings of worthlessness. My addictions to food, diet pills, body image, attention, and unhealthy behaviors probably came from the lack of control that I had felt as a child. I had deep insecurities and believed I could not measure up to the expectations of the world that seemed to constantly judge me.

Although I knew I hadn't had that "fairy tale" childhood, in my late thirties I discovered that my issues with food were more complicated than just body image. I had to treat the "why" of my self-loathing—and I did! I have dealt with adversity, but most importantly, I have overcome so many hardships. I am reaching my goals and following my dreams, one day at a time.

At the age of thirty-nine, I finally started to live. I gained control over my emotions, confronted my fears, and let go of my anger. I gained so much confidence and strength that I now believe anything is possible. Now, at forty years old, I am ready to share my story as I continue helping others achieve their life goals through mindset, balance, strength, fitness, and nutrition. This life is pretty amazing— and it is never too late to start living!

I am a graduate of Winter Haven High School in Winter Haven, Florida. I enlisted in the United States Navy as a Hospital Corpsman in February 1993 but was honorably discharged a few months later when my mother's disease, Multiple Sclerosis, worsened and she had another relapse. In 1996, I attended a nursing program at Pennsylvania College of Technology. In 2003, I began studying exercise science, which I combined with my knowledge or anatomy, physiology, kinesiology, and personal training. I discovered I had a passion for helping others reach their fitness goals.

I began my experience at a local health club where I worked as the fitness director from 2004 to 2010. I then moved to a larger facility where I had room to grow and use my skills. I became General Manager of the Bloomsburg SportsPlex in 2010. My experience, knowledge, and client base blossomed during these years, and I knew it was time to strike out on my own.

In 2014, I became the proud owner of Legacy Fitness Revolution and Personal Training Studio. I hesitated, because the area we live in is saturated with gyms and personal training. However, I knew my programs were changing lives and improving confidence, and my clients were doing things they never expected to do.

My approach to fitness had always been about more than weight loss and appearance. I build confidence and self-esteem. I stepped out of the "norm" with my classes and began to invent my own programs. They worked. I continued with my education and I am still educating myself. I specialize in wellness, weight loss, functional body weight training, strength training, healthy eating, and organic nutrition. I coach, motivate, and empower others to turn their excuses into solutions and become their best possible selves.

I believe the fitness industry offers too many gimmicks and empty promises. Four Season's Fitness Program is designed from knowledge of techniques that have been proven to work.

Being a health and wellness coach has inspired me to combine my skills and study the holistic approach to nutrition and human wellness as well as mental clarity. My Four Seasons Fitness Programs are based on many years of studying, practicing, implementing, and hands-on experience.

I'm ready to expand this knowledge and bring my unique programs and training technique to all of you!

*Education, experience, and certifications: Health and wellness coach, Personal Trainer, and passionate about changing peoples' lives.*

*Certifications: NESTA (National Exercise Sports Trainers Association), NETA, ACE, Youth and Kids Fitness, Zumba, Pilates, Yoga, Personal Training, Club Management, Sports nutrition.*

*Experience: I have worked countless hours training, studying the science of the body, how it works, and why one thing may work for one person but not work for another. Everyone responds differently to nutrition and exercise. My programs work. I coach with confidence, love, compassion, and determination to help others.*

*Education: Pennsylvania State University: Registered Nurse program, Exercise Science. Luzerne County Community College: I studied kinesiology, anatomy, psychology, chemistry, pharmacology, microbiology, and obtained a general studies associate's degree.*

www.charadavisauthor.com

Made in the USA
Lexington, KY
20 November 2016